TEXAS TEST PREP
Practice Test Book
STAAR Reading
Grade 4

© 2014 by Test Master Press Texas

All rights reserved. No part of this book may be reproduced or transmitted in any form or by any means, electronic, mechanical, photocopying, recording, or otherwise without prior written permission.

ISBN 978-1500581459

CONTENTS

Section 1: Reading Mini-Tests   4
     Mini-Test 1: Informational Text   5
     Mini-Test 2: Literary Text   11
     Mini-Test 3: Informational Text   16
     Mini-Test 4: Literary Text   22
     Mini-Test 5: Paired Literary Texts   27
     Mini-Test 6: Paired Informational Texts   33

Section 2: Vocabulary Quizzes   39
     Quiz 1: Use Context to Determine Word Meaning   40
     Quiz 2: Understand and Use Multiple Meaning Words   42
     Quiz 3: Understand and Use Prefixes   44
     Quiz 4: Understand and Use Suffixes   46
     Quiz 5: Use Greek and Latin Roots   48
     Quiz 6: Use a Dictionary or Glossary   50

Section 3: STAAR Reading Practice Test 1   52
     Practice Test 1: Session 1   53
     Practice Test 1: Session 2   66

Section 4: STAAR Reading Practice Test 2   79
     Practice Test 2: Session 1   80
     Practice Test 2: Session 2   94

Answer Key   109
     Section 1: Reading Mini-Tests   110
     Section 2: Vocabulary Quizzes   113
     Section 3: STAAR Reading Practice Test 1   115
     Section 4: STAAR Reading Practice Test 2   117

Multiple Choice Answer Sheets   119
     Section 1: Reading Mini-Tests   119
     Section 2: Vocabulary Quizzes   120
     Section 3: STAAR Reading Practice Test 1   121
     Section 4: STAAR Reading Practice Test 2   122

Section 1: Reading Mini-Tests

INTRODUCTION TO THE READING MINI-TESTS
For Parents, Teachers, and Tutors

How Reading is Assessed by the State of Texas

The STAAR Reading test assesses reading skills by having students read passages and answer questions about the passages. On the STAAR Reading test, students read 4 or 5 literary or informational passages, as well as 1 or 2 sets of paired passages. Students answer a total of 42 multiple-choice questions.

About the Reading Mini-Tests

This section of the practice test book contains passages and question sets similar to those on the STAAR Reading tests. However, students can take mini-tests instead of taking a complete practice test. Each mini-test has either one literary passage, one informational passage, or a set of paired passages. Students answer 10 multiple-choice questions about the passage or passages.

This section of the book is an effective way for students to build up to taking the full-length test. Students can focus on one passage or pair of passages and a small set of questions at a time. This will build confidence and help students become familiar with answering test questions. Students will gradually develop the skills they need to complete the full-length practice tests in Section 3 and Section 4 of this book.

Reading Skills

The STAAR Reading test assesses a specific set of skills. These skills are described in the TEKS, or Texas Essential Knowledge and Skills. The full answer key at the end of the book identifies the specific skill that each question is testing.

STAAR READING

Mini-Test 1

Informational Text

Instructions

This set has one passage for you to read. Read the passage and answer the questions that follow it.

Choose the best answer to each question. Then fill in the circle for the best answer.

The Sahara Desert

The Sahara Desert is the world's largest subtropical desert. It covers most of North Africa. Its area is about 3.5 million square miles. This makes it almost as large as the United States of America. The Sahara Desert stretches all the way across Africa.

The Sahara Desert divides the continent of Africa into north and south. The southern border is marked by a savannah known as the Sahel. The land that lies to the south of the savannah is lush with more vegetation. The Sahara Desert features many large sand dunes. Some of these measure more than 600 feet from base to peak.

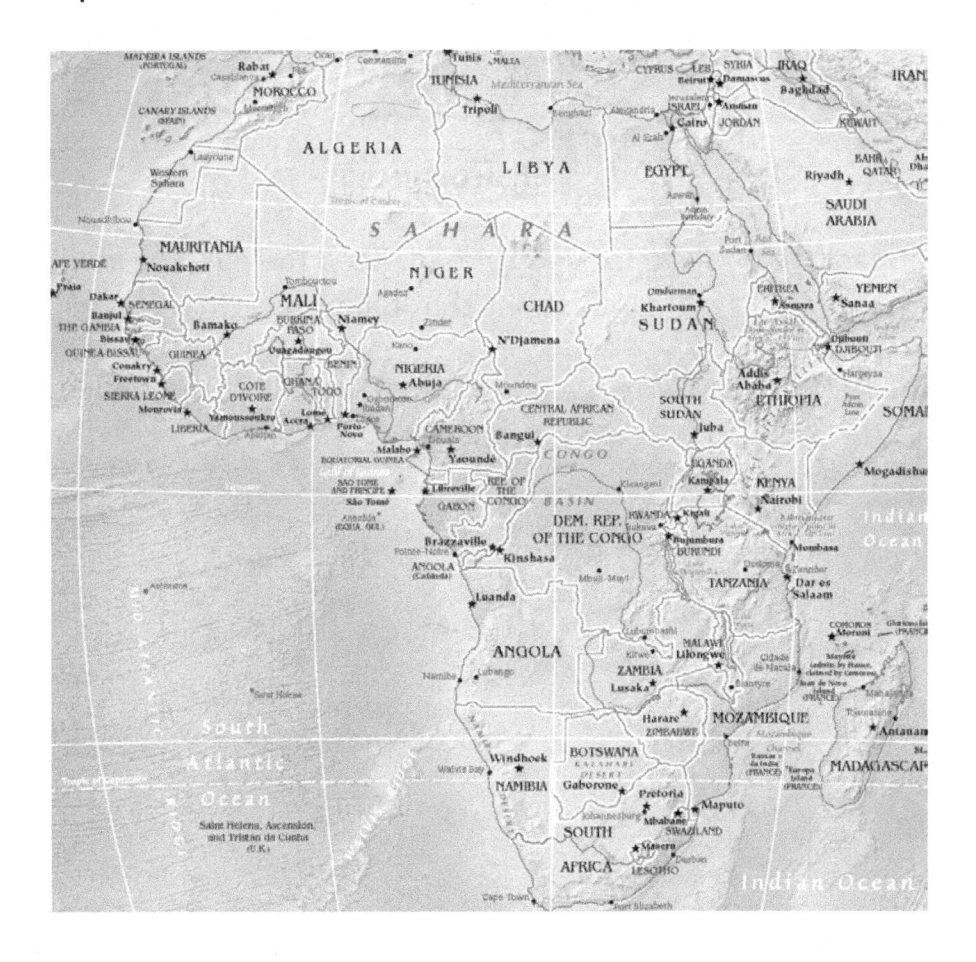

The Sahara Desert has been largely dry and with little plant life for more than 5,000 years. Before this time, it was far wetter than it is today. This allowed more plant life to thrive across its land. Thousands of ancient engravings have been found that show many types of river animals have lived in the Sahara Desert. These have been found mainly in southeast Algeria. These suggest that crocodiles lived in the region at some point in time.

The climate of the Sahara Desert has changed over several thousands of years. The area is also far smaller than it was during the last ice age. It was the end of the last ice age that brought a high level of rainfall to the Sahara. This was between 8000 and 6000 BC. Since this time, the northern part of the Sahara has gradually dried out. Though the southern Sahara still receives rain during monsoon season, it is still far less than years before. Some of the tallest mountain ranges occasionally receive snow peaks. The Tibetsi Mountains record some level of snowfall about once every seven years.

The modern era has seen several developments for the Sahara. One of these is that mines have been built to get the most from the natural resources within the region. There are also plans to build several highways across the Sahara. It is expected that one of these may be completed at some point in the future.

1   Read this sentence from the passage.

   The Sahara Desert stretches all the way across Africa.

   Why does the author most likely use the phrase "stretches all the way across"?

   - Ⓐ   To emphasize how wide the desert is
   - Ⓑ   To suggest that the desert is always changing
   - Ⓒ   To show that the desert is mainly flat
   - Ⓓ   To indicate that the desert has always been there

2   Read this sentence from the passage.

   The Sahara Desert is the world's largest subtropical desert.

   What does the prefix in the word <u>subtropical</u> mean?

   - Ⓐ   Just outside of
   - Ⓑ   The opposite of
   - Ⓒ   Between or among
   - Ⓓ   More than

3   Which sentence from the passage is best supported by the map?
   - Ⓐ   *The Sahara Desert is the world's largest subtropical desert.*
   - Ⓑ   *The Sahara Desert stretches all the way across Africa.*
   - Ⓒ   *The Sahara Desert features many large sand dunes.*
   - Ⓓ   *The Sahara Desert has been largely dry and with little plant life for more than 5,000 years.*

Practice Test Book, STAAR Reading, Grade 4

4 According to the passage, how was the Sahara Desert different thousands of years ago?

- Ⓐ It had fewer animals.
- Ⓑ It was wetter.
- Ⓒ It had smaller sand dunes.
- Ⓓ It was home to fewer people.

5 Which of the following is most similar about the Sahara Desert and the United States?

- Ⓐ Its size
- Ⓑ Its climate
- Ⓒ Its uses
- Ⓓ Its location

6 Where would this passage most likely be found?

- Ⓐ In an encyclopedia
- Ⓑ In an atlas
- Ⓒ In a history textbook
- Ⓓ In a book of short stories

7 How is the fourth paragraph of the passage organized?

- Ⓐ A problem is described and then a solution is given.
- Ⓑ The cause of an event is described.
- Ⓒ A claim is made and then details are given to support it.
- Ⓓ A question is asked and then answered.

8 Based on the map, which country completes the chart below?

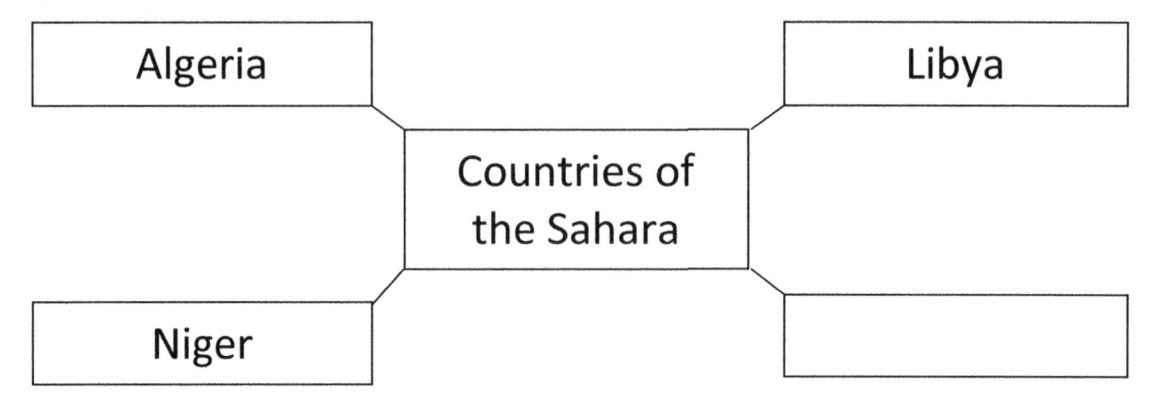

```
┌─────────┐                    ┌─────────┐
│ Algeria │                    │  Libya  │
└─────────┘                    └─────────┘
         ┌──────────────────┐
         │   Countries of   │
         │    the Sahara    │
         └──────────────────┘
┌─────────┐                    ┌─────────┐
│  Niger  │                    │         │
└─────────┘                    └─────────┘
```

- Ⓐ Angola
- Ⓑ Chad
- Ⓒ Tanzania
- Ⓓ Zambia

9 Which sentence would make the best caption for the photograph?

- Ⓐ *The Sahara Desert stretches all the way across Africa.*
- Ⓑ *The Sahara Desert divides the continent of Africa into north and south.*
- Ⓒ *The Sahara Desert features many large sand dunes.*
- Ⓓ *The climate of the Sahara Desert has changed over several thousands of years.*

10 Which of these describes a modern development of the Sahara?

- Ⓐ Tourist attractions have been created.
- Ⓑ Major cities have developed.
- Ⓒ Rail lines have been added.
- Ⓓ Mines have been built.

STAAR READING

Mini-Test 2

Literary Text

Instructions

This set has one passage for you to read. Read the passage and answer the questions that follow it.

Choose the best answer to each question. Then fill in the circle for the best answer.

The Girlfriend and the Mother

Prince Arnold had a very close bond with his mother. They shared everything with each other. They had remained close since he had been a child. One day, he met a girl named Chloe and she became his girlfriend. Gradually, Arnold began to spend more time with his girlfriend than with his mother.

Although he still enjoyed long conversations with his mother, she began to feel left out. She felt that the only time she would get to spend with him was in the evenings. This was when he would fall asleep on the couch and she would sit beside him and stroke his hair.

His mother really liked the gray strands that grew in his hair. She felt they made him look wise. So as she stroked his head she would remove some of the darker hairs from his scalp. She did this over many nights for an entire year.

Arnold's girlfriend had a similar habit. She thought that his gray hairs made him look old. So she would pluck as many gray hairs from his head as she possibly could. She too did this for many nights over the year.

After a year had gone by, Arnold found that he was almost completely bald. His mother and girlfriend had removed so much of his hair that he was left only with short little tufts. Both women and Arnold were unhappy with his new look. The ladies felt that their battle for his time had led to the problem.

"We're so sorry," they said. "What we have done is unfair."

They realized that they must all get along and spend time together if they were to remain happy. The mother and the girlfriend made a promise to be happy sharing Prince Arnold's time.

Practice Test Book, STAAR Reading, Grade 4

1   What does the word <u>removed</u> mean in the sentence below?

His mother and girlfriend had removed so much of his hair that he was left only with short little tufts.

- Ⓐ   Scared off
- Ⓑ   Fought over
- Ⓒ   Taken away
- Ⓓ   Changed places

2   Which meaning of the word <u>bond</u> is used in the sentence below?

Prince Arnold had a very close bond with his mother.

- Ⓐ   To connect two or more items
- Ⓑ   A relationship or link between people
- Ⓒ   An agreement or promise
- Ⓓ   A type of glue

3   What is the mother's main problem in the passage?
- Ⓐ   She dislikes her son's hair.
- Ⓑ   She does not want to share her son.
- Ⓒ   She argues with her son.
- Ⓓ   She wants her son to get married.

4 "The Girlfriend and the Mother" is most like a —

- Ⓐ true story
- Ⓑ science fiction story
- Ⓒ biography
- Ⓓ fable

5 How are the girlfriend and the mother alike?

- Ⓐ They are both pleased when Arnold is bald.
- Ⓑ They both pluck out Arnold's hair.
- Ⓒ They both dislike Arnold's gray hair.
- Ⓓ They have both known Arnold since he was young.

6 How does the mother change in the passage?

- Ⓐ She realizes that her son is a grown man.
- Ⓑ She accepts her son's relationship with Chloe.
- Ⓒ She loses interest in her son.
- Ⓓ She learns that Chloe is a nice person.

7 According to the passage, Chloe thinks that Arnold's gray hair makes him look —

- Ⓐ wise
- Ⓑ royal
- Ⓒ old
- Ⓓ kind

8 What will the mother most likely do next?

    Ⓐ   Come up with a plan to break up her son and Chloe

    ~~Ⓑ~~   Start making an effort to spend time with her son and Chloe

    Ⓒ   Make her son think that his baldness is Chloe's fault

    Ⓓ   Start spending time with her husband instead of her son

9 Which sentence completes the empty box in the diagram below?

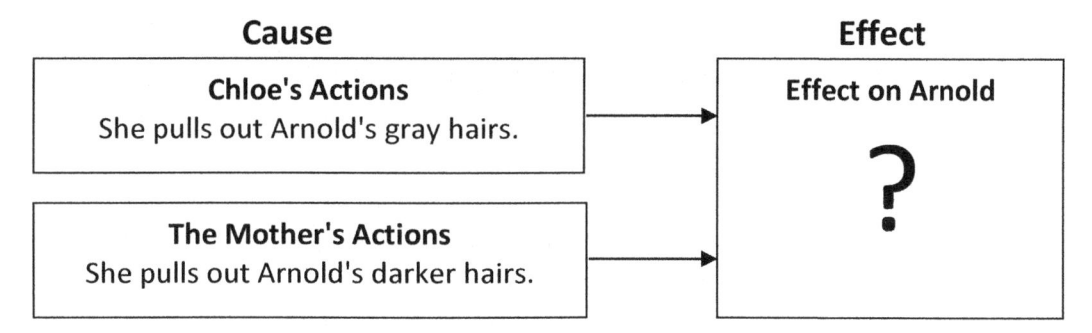

Cause	Effect
Chloe's Actions She pulls out Arnold's gray hairs.	**Effect on Arnold** **?**
The Mother's Actions She pulls out Arnold's darker hairs.	

    Ⓐ   Arnold refuses to speak to his mother.

    ~~Ⓑ~~   Arnold loses almost all of his hair.

    Ⓒ   Arnold worries about his future.

    Ⓓ   Arnold makes his wife and mother make up.

10 Who is telling the story?

    Ⓐ   Chloe

    Ⓑ   Arnold

    Ⓒ   Arnold's mother

    ~~Ⓓ~~   Someone not in the story

STAAR READING

Mini-Test 3

Informational Text

Instructions

This set has one passage for you to read. Read the passage and answer the questions that follow it.

Choose the best answer to each question. Then fill in the circle for the best answer.

Grooming a King Charles Cavalier

The King Charles Cavalier is a small breed of Spaniel dog. It is known as a toy dog by kennel clubs. They are very popular in the United States and around the world. These dogs have a silky coat and can be difficult to groom. Professional groomers can carry out the task. However, many owners choose to save money and groom their dog themselves. It takes some patience, but you can learn to groom a King Charles Cavalier.

Start by making sure you have the correct equipment to groom your dog correctly. You will need:
- a comb
- a brush
- dog-friendly conditioner

You should complete these steps when your dog is clean. If your dog's coat is dirty, give the dog a bath first. Then dry the coat before starting.

Step 1
Before you start, make sure that your dog is in a comfortable position either on your lap or on a blanket. Your dog should be nice and relaxed.

Step 2
Take your comb and move it smoothly through the coat. There may be some knots or tangles, so be sure not to comb it too fast. You don't want to pull at the dog's fur, cause your dog any discomfort, or scare it. Be gentle, but make sure that all dead or matted hair is removed.

Step 3
Once the combing is complete, add some of the conditioner to the coat. This will add shine and make it easier to brush your dog.

Step 4
Comb your dog's coat for a second time to make sure that it is as smooth as it can be.

Step 5

It is now time to brush your King Charles Cavalier. Keep a firm hold on the brush and be sure to keep your dog still. Move the brush gently through your dog's coat. Take care to smooth out any lumps or patches of uneven hair. Move through each area of the coat twice.

Step 6

Once you've finished brushing, condition your dogs coat again. This helps to keep your dog's coat free from tangles. It will also make it easier to groom your dog in the future.

Step 7

Lastly, all you need to do is gently pat the dog's coat dry. Your dog is now nicely groomed and the coat should stay that way for around 4 to 6 weeks.

You can give your dog a small food reward after you've finished the grooming. This will help make sure your dog looks forward to being groomed.

1   Read this dictionary entry for the word firm.

> **firm** *adjective*
> 1. solid or hard when pressed 2. showing determination 3. secure and unlikely to give way 4. unlikely to change

Which definition of the word firm is used in the sentence below?

Keep a firm hold on the brush and be sure to keep your dog still.

- Ⓐ Definition 1
- Ⓑ Definition 2
- Ⓒ Definition 3
- Ⓓ Definition 4

2   In the sentence below, what does the word silky mainly describe?

These dogs have a silky coat and can be difficult to groom.

- Ⓐ How long the coat is
- Ⓑ How the coat feels
- Ⓒ What the coat smells like
- Ⓓ What color the coat is

3   In which step is the conditioner first needed?
- Ⓐ Step 1
- Ⓑ Step 3
- Ⓒ Step 5
- Ⓓ Step 7

4 Which of these is NOT a reason for adding conditioner?

- Ⓐ To add shine to the coat
- Ⓑ To stop the coat from getting tangles
- **Ⓒ** To prevent the dog from getting fleas
- Ⓓ To make it easier to brush the dog

5 What is the main purpose of the passage?

- **Ⓐ** To teach readers how to do something
- Ⓑ To entertain readers with a story
- Ⓒ To inform readers about a type of dog
- Ⓓ To compare different types of dog products

6 What is the purpose of the bullet points?

- Ⓐ To describe the steps
- Ⓑ To give useful hints
- Ⓒ To list the items needed
- **Ⓓ** To highlight the key points

7 Which detail from the photograph is most relevant to the passage?

- Ⓐ The size of the dog
- Ⓑ The color of the dog
- **Ⓒ** The look of the dog's fur
- Ⓓ The look on the dog's face

8 According to the passage, what should you do right after brushing the dog?

  Ⓐ Condition the dog's coat
  Ⓑ Comb the dog's coat a second time
  Ⓒ Rinse the dog's coat
  Ⓓ Give the dog a treat

9 In the sentence below, what does the word <u>discomfort</u> mean?

  You don't want to pull at the dog's fur, cause your dog any discomfort, or scare it.

  Ⓐ Excitement
  Ⓑ Calm
  Ⓒ Embarrassment
  Ⓓ Pain

10 The author states that it takes patience to groom a King Charles Cavalier. Which of these sentences from the passage best explains why patience is important?

  Ⓐ *Before you start, make sure that your dog is in a comfortable position either on your lap or on a blanket.*
  Ⓑ *There may be some knots or tangles, so be sure not to comb it too fast.*
  Ⓒ *Once the combing is complete, add some of the conditioner to the coat.*
  Ⓓ *You can give your dog a small food reward after you've finished the grooming.*

STAAR READING

Mini-Test 4

Literary Text

Instructions

This set has one passage for you to read. Read the passage and answer the questions that follow it.

Choose the best answer to each question. Then fill in the circle for the best answer.

The Taming of the Lion

Free verse

1 The lion had a fearful roar
2 that scared all who dared to follow.
3 It made his victims run and hide,
4 and pray for their tomorrow.

5 His mane was as glorious as sunshine,
6 and framed his handsome face.
7 His lair was known to all around
8 as a truly frightening place.

9 Until he met a maiden,
10 and fell hopelessly in love.
11 His roar became a whisper,
12 a soft sound to birds above.

13 His lair was soon a palace,
14 a kindly home of gentle calm,
15 where he would hold his loved ones,
16 and make sure they met no harm.

17 The lion never harmed another,
18 or chased his worried prey.
19 Instead they lived in harmony
20 and shared each summer's day.

21 He had been tamed within an instant
22 by the gentle hand of love,
23 that would keep him calm forever
24 beneath the flight of gentle doves.

Practice Test Book, STAAR Reading, Grade 4

1   In the line below, what does the word <u>fearful</u> mean?

The lion had a fearful roar

- Ⓐ   Without fear
- Ⓑ   Having fear
- Ⓒ   More fear
- Ⓓ   Less fear

2   According to the poem, why does the lion become tamer?
- Ⓐ   He gets older.
- Ⓑ   He falls in love.
- Ⓒ   He has children.
- Ⓓ   He starts feeling lonely.

3   What is the rhyme pattern of each stanza of the poem?
- Ⓐ   The second and fourth lines rhyme.
- Ⓑ   There are two pairs of rhyming lines.
- Ⓒ   The first and last lines rhyme.
- Ⓓ   None of the lines rhyme.

4   Which line from the poem contains a simile?
- Ⓐ   *His mane was as glorious as sunshine,*
- Ⓑ   *and framed his handsome face.*
- Ⓒ   *His lair was known to all around*
- Ⓓ   *as a truly frightening place.*

5   Which statement best summarizes the events of the poem?

   Ⓐ   A humorous character becomes serious.

   Ⓑ   A selfish character becomes giving.

   Ⓒ   A tough character becomes weak.

   ● Ⓓ   A feared character becomes calmer.

6   Read this line from the poem.

   a soft sound to birds above

   The alliteration in this line mainly creates a feeling of —

   Ⓐ   uneasiness

   Ⓑ   surprise

   ● Ⓒ   calm

   Ⓓ   fear

7   Read this line from the poem.

   His roar became a whisper,

   What does this change show about the lion?

   Ⓐ   He has become shy.

   ● Ⓑ   He is no longer scary.

   Ⓒ   He feels afraid.

   Ⓓ   He listens to others.

8 The poem states that the lion had been tamed "within an instant." What does the phrase "within an instant" mean?

- Ⓐ Very well
- Ⓑ Unusually
- **Ⓒ Suddenly**
- Ⓓ Over a long time

9 What does the imagery in the lines below help the reader understand?

> **It made his victims run and hide,
> and pray for their tomorrow.**

- Ⓐ Where the lion lives
- Ⓑ How feared the lion is
- Ⓒ Why the lion dislikes people
- **Ⓓ How strong and fast the lion is**

10 Which pair of lines from the poem explain what causes the lion to change?

- Ⓐ *His mane was as glorious as sunshine,
  and framed his handsome face.*
- **Ⓑ *Until he met a maiden,
  and fell hopelessly in love.***
- Ⓒ *His lair was soon a palace,
  a kindly home of gentle calm,*
- Ⓓ *The lion never harmed another,
  or chased his worried prey.*

STAAR READING

Mini-Test 5

Paired Literary Texts

Instructions

This set has two passages for you to read. Read both passages. Then answer the questions about the passages.

Choose the best answer to each question. Then fill in the circle for the best answer.

Directions: Read the next two passages. Then answer the questions.

Disappearing Dessert

It was a windy autumn morning in the backstreets of Brooklyn, New York. Tony was walking to the barber shop carrying a brown paper bag filled with cannolis. Along the way, he stopped to talk with Vinnie at the newspaper stand and gave him a few cannolis. Tony said his goodbyes and continued on toward the barber shop.

He had nearly arrived when he ran into Jen. The two spoke for a while and Tony gave Jen a handful of cannolis to eat for dessert that evening. Just around the corner from the barber shop, he saw Mr. Jackson walking his dog. He raced over to say hello, and then offered Mr. Jackson a cannoli.

Tony finally made it to the barber shop.

"Uncle Benny! Here are the delicious cannolis you asked Mamma to make for you!" Tony exclaimed.

He handed over the brown paper bag to his Uncle Benny and left the shop to go back home. Uncle Benny looked into the bag to find nothing inside.

"Crazy boy, there are no cannolis in here," he grumbled.

©John Mueller

The Cookie Thief

Max was sitting at his desk early one morning flipping wildly through the pages of his notebook and pinning up hastily written notes on his corkboard. Max had covered his entire corkboard with clues, and drawn maps of his house. He paced back and forth, stared at the board, and then remembered something else. He scribbled something on another piece of note paper and added it to the board.

"I'm going to find out who ate my cookies if it's the last thing I do!" Max said as he worked away on his investigation. Max's dog Lucky just stared up at him.

Max jumped up and headed for his sister's room. Along with his father, she was the main suspect. Before he had even set foot outside of his room, Max tripped on something, stumbled, and fell. Max sat up and shook himself off. He looked around to see what he had tripped on. Right in front of him was a plastic bowl filled with cookie crumbs. Max suddenly remembered that he'd snuck out in the middle of the night for a snack. He was suddenly glad that he hadn't stormed in and blamed his sister for something she hadn't done.

Directions: Use "Disappearing Dessert" to answer the following questions.

1. Which detail from the passage best shows that Tony is generous?
   - Ⓐ He stops to talk to everyone he knows.
   - ● He offers to give everyone cannolis.
   - Ⓒ Uncle Benny calls him a crazy boy.
   - Ⓓ He bakes cannolis for his friends.

2. Who is telling the story?
   - Ⓐ Tony
   - Ⓑ Uncle Benny
   - Ⓒ Mr. Jackson
   - ● An outside narrator

3. What happened to the cannolis?
   - ● Tony gave them away.
   - Ⓑ They fell out of the bag.
   - Ⓒ Mamma didn't put any in the bag.
   - Ⓓ Tony ate them as he was walking.

4. What information does the photograph offer the reader?
   - Ⓐ It shows how many cannolis Tony had.
   - Ⓑ It shows why Uncle Benny asked for cannolis.
   - ● It shows what a cannoli is.
   - Ⓓ It shows what happened to the cannolis.

Directions: Use "The Cookie Thief" to answer the following questions.

5 Which sentence from the passage shows the main lesson that Max learns?

- Ⓐ *Max had covered his entire corkboard with clues, and drawn maps of his house.*
- Ⓑ *I'm going to find out who ate my cookies if it's the last thing I do!*
- ● *Max suddenly remembered that he'd snuck out in the middle of the night for a snack.*
- Ⓓ *He was suddenly glad that he hadn't stormed in and blamed his sister for something she hadn't done.*

6 What happens right after Max sees the bowl of cookie crumbs?

- Ⓐ He trips over something.
- Ⓑ He decides that his sister is to blame.
- ● He remembers how he snacked the night before.
- ● He starts to investigate the missing cookies.

7 Read this dictionary entry for the word <u>suspect</u>.

> **suspect**
> *verb* 1. to believe someone to be guilty 2. to mistrust someone 3. to believe that something is likely
> *noun* 4. a person who is thought to have done something wrong

Which definition of the word <u>suspect</u> is used in the sentence below?

Along with his father, she was the main suspect.

- ● Definition 1
- Ⓑ Definition 2
- Ⓒ Definition 3
- Ⓓ Definition 4

Directions: Use both "Disappearing Dessert" and "The Cookie Thief" to answer the following questions.

8 What is the main way the two passages are similar?

   Ⓐ They both describe a boy playing a trick.

   Ⓑ They both involve a missing food item.

   Ⓒ They both explain why people like treats.

   Ⓓ They both show how getting angry achieves nothing.

9 How is the ending of "The Cookie Thief" different from the ending of "Disappearing Dessert"?

   Ⓐ Max realizes his mistake, while Tony does not.

   Ⓑ Max becomes angry, while Tony remains calm.

   Ⓒ Max makes up for his mistake, while Tony makes more mistakes.

   Ⓓ Max feels proud of himself, while Tony feels embarrassed.

10 Both passages have a third-person point of view. How is the third-person point of view different in "The Cookie Thief" than in "Disappearing (two) Dessert"?

   Ⓐ The author gives more opinions on Max's actions.

   Ⓑ The author includes more details that show Max's feelings.

   Ⓒ The author describes how other characters view Max.

   Ⓓ The author includes personal opinions on Max's actions.

STAAR READING

Mini-Test 6

Paired Informational Texts

Instructions

This set has two passages for you to read. Read both passages. Then answer the questions about the passages.

Choose the best answer to each question. Then fill in the circle for the best answer.

Directions: Read the next two passages. Then answer the questions.

Mozart

Mozart is a famous German composer of the classical era. His full name was Wolfgang Amadeus Mozart and he was born in 1756. He has composed over 600 pieces of classical music. These include works for the piano and violin, as well as whole operas.

Mozart began composing at the age of 5. At this time, he wrote small pieces for his father. He continued to learn and write music all through his youth. When he was 17, he worked as a court musician in Austria. He was given the opportunity to write a range of musical pieces.

Mozart left Austria in search of better work, and lived in Paris for over a year. During this time, he was unable to find work, but he still continued writing music.

He then moved to Vienna. Mozart wrote most of his best-known work while living in Vienna. He wrote operas, performed in concerts, produced concerts, and performed solos. He gained both money and fame and was able to live very well for a short time. However, he lived too lavishly and his income could not keep up with his spending. Much of his later years were spent struggling to support his family and to pay off his debts. He died at the age of 35 in 1791.

As well as his major works, he is remembered for inspiring later composers. Other famous composers including Beethoven and Hummel studied his work and learned from it. Even today, music students all over the world continue to study and perform his work. His operas and symphonies are still performed today.

Michelangelo

Born in 1475, Michelangelo was a genius of both academics and artistry. He lived during the Renaissance, which was a time in Europe when art was thriving. He was considered a typical Renaissance man. This term refers to people who have talents in many different areas. While he is best known as an artist and sculptor, he was also a poet, an engineer, and an architect.

Michelangelo's work became renowned pieces of the period in which he lived. The Statue of David, completed in 1504, is arguably one of Michelangelo's most famous works. It was sculpted from marble, and took over two years to complete. It is still respected and admired today.

A less known fact about the statue is that it was originally intended to be placed on the roof of the Florence Cathedral. Just before it was complete, people realized that placing it on the Florence Cathedral would be impossible. The statue weighed over 6 ton. While the roof would probably be able to support the weight, it would have been almost impossible to lift the statue to put it up there. This was in the 1500s before cranes and other machinery would have made the task a lot simpler! The statue was placed in a public square in Florence instead. It can be found today at the Academy of Fine Arts in Florence. Visitors to Florence can also see a replica of the famous statue where it was originally placed.

A close-up view of The Statue of David shows the striking detail of the sculpture.

Directions: Use "Mozart" to answer the following questions.

1. In the sentence below, what does the word <u>composed</u> most likely refer to?

   He has composed over 600 pieces of classical music.

   - Ⓐ Playing a song
   - Ⓑ Writing a song
   - Ⓒ Singing a song
   - Ⓓ Listening to a song

2. What type of passage is "Mozart"?
   - Ⓐ Realistic fiction
   - Ⓑ Biography
   - Ⓒ Autobiography
   - Ⓓ Fable

3. If the passage were given another title, which title would best fit?
   - Ⓐ The Life of a Great Composer
   - Ⓑ How to Compose Music
   - Ⓒ Living in Austria
   - Ⓓ Learn the Piano Today

4. In which location did Mozart complete his most important works?
   - Ⓐ Austria
   - Ⓑ Germany
   - Ⓒ Paris
   - Ⓓ Vienna

Directions: Use "Michelangelo" to answer the following questions.

5. What does the close-up view of The Statue of David best help readers understand?
   - Ⓐ Why the statue was so heavy
   - Ⓑ Why the statue lasted so long
   - Ⓒ Why the statue took so long to complete
   - Ⓓ Why the statue was placed in a public square

6. In the first paragraph, the word thriving shows that art was —
   - Ⓐ costly
   - Ⓑ varied
   - Ⓒ disliked
   - Ⓓ popular

7. Which sentence best supports the idea that Michelangelo was a "typical Renaissance man"?
   - Ⓐ *This term refers to people who have talents in many different areas.*
   - Ⓑ *While he is best known as an artist and sculptor, he was also a poet, an engineer, and an architect.*
   - Ⓒ *Michelangelo's work became renowned pieces of the period in which he lived.*
   - Ⓓ *The Statue of David, completed in 1504, is arguably one of Michelangelo's most famous works.*

Directions: Use both "Mozart" and "Michelangelo" to answer the following questions.

8   Based on the passages, both Mozart and Michelangelo could be described as —

　Ⓐ   talented
　Ⓑ   unlucky
　Ⓒ   foolish
　Ⓓ   determined

9   Which of these describes one difference between the passages "Mozart" and "Michelangelo"?

　Ⓐ   "Mozart" explains why the person achieved such success.
　Ⓑ   "Mozart" encourages people to value the works completed.
　Ⓒ   "Mozart" shows that the person is still remembered today.
　Ⓓ   "Mozart" describes the person's difficulties as well as achievements.

10   Which of these describes a main purpose of both passages?

　Ⓐ   To encourage people not to give up on their dreams
　Ⓑ   To inform people about the life and works of a person
　Ⓒ   To persuade people to study the works of famous people
　Ⓓ   To teach people about the history of Europe

Section 2: Vocabulary Quizzes

INTRODUCTION TO THE VOCABULARY QUIZZES
For Parents, Teachers, and Tutors

How Vocabulary is Assessed by the State of Texas

The STAAR Reading test includes multiple-choice questions that assess vocabulary skills. These questions follow each passage and are mixed in with the reading comprehension questions.

These questions require students to complete the following tasks:
- use context to determine the meaning of unfamiliar words
- use context to determine the meaning of multiple meaning words
- determine the meaning of words with suffixes
- determine the meaning of words with prefixes
- determine the meaning of words derived from Latin and Greek roots or affixes
- use a dictionary or glossary to determine the meaning, syllabication, and pronunciation of unknown words

About the Vocabulary Quizzes

This section of the practice test book contains six quizzes. Each quiz tests one vocabulary skill that is covered on the state test.

This section of the book covers all of the vocabulary skills assessed on the STAAR Reading test. The aim of the quizzes is to help ensure that students have all the vocabulary skills that they will need for the STAAR Reading test. If students can master this section of the book, they will be ready to answer the vocabulary questions.

Quiz 1: Use Context to Determine Word Meaning

1 What does the word <u>ashamed</u> mean in the sentence below?

Karl felt ashamed of the mess he had made.

- Ⓐ   Proud
- **Ⓑ**   Embarrassed
- Ⓒ   Worried
- Ⓓ   Pleased

2 What does the word <u>entire</u> mean in the sentence below?

After the storm, the entire yard was covered with snow.

- **Ⓐ**   Whole
- Ⓑ   Large
- Ⓒ   Cold
- Ⓓ   Outside

3 Why does the author use the word <u>swooped</u> in the sentence?

The bird swooped down and picked up the worm.

- Ⓐ   To show that the bird looked beautiful
- Ⓑ   To show that the bird was flying
- **Ⓒ**   To show that the bird moved quickly downwards
- Ⓓ   To show that the bird was clumsy

4 What does the word expert show in the sentence below?

Josh read many books and became an expert on snakes.

- Ⓐ Josh knew a lot about snakes.
- Ⓑ Josh was not afraid of snakes.
- Ⓒ Josh owned snakes.
- Ⓓ Josh liked snakes very much.

5 What does the word exchange mean in the sentence below?

Mandy decided to exchange the dress for another.

- Ⓐ Make
- Ⓑ Buy
- Ⓒ Swap
- Ⓓ Sell

6 What does the word silent show?

Carrie was alone in the woods and everything was silent.

- Ⓐ There was nobody else around.
- Ⓑ There was no noise.
- Ⓒ There was very little light.
- Ⓓ There was a problem.

Quiz 2: Understand and Use Multiple Meaning Words

1. If an object is <u>rocketing</u> through the air, it is —

    Ⓐ letting off flames

    Ⓑ traveling upwards

    Ⓒ spinning around

    Ⓓ moving very quickly

2. In which sentence does <u>type</u> mean the same as below?

    Kent asked Penny what <u>type</u> of cake she wanted.

    Ⓐ It took Allan a long time to <u>type</u> the letter.

    Ⓑ The <u>type</u> on the old newspaper made it hard to read.

    Ⓒ Anna said that Morgan was not her <u>type</u>.

    Ⓓ Kyle couldn't decide what <u>type</u> of car to buy.

3. What does the word <u>rose</u> mean in the sentence?

    The people in the crowd rose and started clapping.

    Ⓐ Stood up

    Ⓑ Moved higher

    Ⓒ Developed

    Ⓓ Puffed up

4. How is <u>shoving</u> a person different from <u>pushing</u> a person?
   - Ⓐ The person is pushed over.
   - **Ⓑ** The person is pushed roughly.
   - Ⓒ The person is pushed lightly.
   - Ⓓ The person is pushed gently.

5. Which word can be used to complete both sentences?

   The summer day was sunny and _warm_.
   Jacob got a _clear_ for parking his car on the curb.

   - **Ⓐ** clear
   - Ⓑ fine
   - **Ⓒ** warm
   - Ⓓ speech

6. What does the word <u>sink</u> mean in the sentence below?

   The old boat started to sink below the waves.

   - **Ⓐ** To go under
   - Ⓑ A bowl or basin
   - Ⓒ To become worse
   - Ⓓ To dig or drill

Quiz 3: Understand and Use Prefixes

1. What does the word <u>recharge</u> mean?
   - Ⓐ Charge more
   - Ⓑ Not charge
   - Ⓒ Charge before
   - **Ⓓ Charge again**

2. Which prefix can be added to the word <u>spell</u> to make a word meaning "spell incorrectly"?
   - Ⓐ pre-
   - Ⓑ non-
   - **Ⓒ mis-**
   - Ⓓ dis-

3. What does the word <u>nonstop</u> mean?
   - **Ⓐ Without stopping**
   - Ⓑ Stopping once
   - Ⓒ Stopping often
   - Ⓓ Stopping first

4. Which prefix can be added to the word <u>fair</u> to make a word meaning "not fair"?
   - **Ⓐ un-**
   - Ⓑ in-
   - Ⓒ mis-
   - Ⓓ dis-

5   Which word means "pay before"?
    - Ⓐ Prepay
    - Ⓑ Repay
    - Ⓒ Mispay
    - Ⓓ Unpay

6   Which prefix should be added to the word to make the sentence correct?

    The dog ___ obeyed George and ran off.

    - Ⓐ un-
    - Ⓑ dis-
    - Ⓒ in-
    - Ⓓ mis-

7   If an item in a store is <u>inexpensive</u>, it is –
    - Ⓐ costly
    - Ⓑ cheap
    - Ⓒ new
    - Ⓓ used

8   Which word means "very happy"?
    - Ⓐ Enjoy
    - Ⓑ Overjoyed
    - Ⓒ Joyless
    - Ⓓ Underjoyed

Quiz 4: Understand and Use Suffixes

1. What does the word <u>sweetest</u> mean?

   Ⓐ Not sweet

   Ⓑ More sweet

   Ⓒ The most sweet

   Ⓓ In a way that is sweet

2. Which suffix can be added to the word <u>fault</u> to make a word meaning "without fault"?

   Ⓐ -less

   Ⓑ -ful

   Ⓒ -ing

   Ⓓ -ed

3. Which word means "one who performs magic"?

   Ⓐ Magical

   Ⓑ Magician

   Ⓒ Magically

   Ⓓ Magicless

4. If a scratch on a car door is described as <u>noticeable</u>, it —

   Ⓐ is hidden from view

   Ⓑ has been there a long time

   Ⓒ cannot be removed

   Ⓓ can be seen

Practice Test Book, STAAR Reading, Grade 4

5   Which suffix should be added to the word to make the sentence correct?

   The cave was in total dark_____.

   Ⓐ   -ful
   Ⓑ   -est
   Ⓒ   -ness
   Ⓓ   -er

6   What does the word <u>flavorful</u> mean?

   Ⓐ   Having flavor
   Ⓑ   The most flavor
   Ⓒ   The act of flavoring
   Ⓓ   Lacking flavor

7   Which suffix can be added to the word <u>cloud</u> to make a word meaning "full of clouds"?

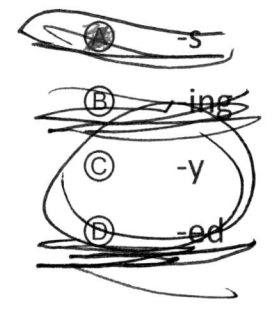

   Ⓐ   -s
   Ⓑ   -ing
   Ⓒ   -y
   Ⓓ   -ed

8   In which word is the suffix –er used?

   Ⓐ   Reindeer
   Ⓑ   Butler
   Ⓒ   Darker
   Ⓓ   Sister

Quiz 5: Use Greek and Latin Roots

1. The word <u>aquatic</u> contains the Latin root <u>aqua-</u>. An <u>aquatic</u> plant is probably one that —

    Ⓐ lives on land

    Ⓑ lives in water

    Ⓒ needs sunlight

    Ⓓ has flowers

2. The Latin root <u>glaci-</u> is used in the word <u>glacier</u>. What does the Latin root <u>glaci-</u> mean?

    Ⓐ Cold

    Ⓑ Ice

    Ⓒ Far

    Ⓓ Water

3. The word <u>spectator</u> is based on the Latin root <u>spect-</u>, which means "watch or look at." Based on this, what is a <u>spectator</u>?

    Ⓐ Someone who looks good

    Ⓑ Someone who is watching something

    Ⓒ Someone who knows the time

    Ⓓ Someone who wears glasses

4 The word monotone contains the Greek root mono-. What does the word monotone mean?

- Ⓐ One tone
- Ⓑ Two tones
- **Ⓒ Many tones**
- Ⓓ More tones

5 The Greek root oct- is used in the word octopus. What does the Greek root oct- mean?

- Ⓐ Ocean
- Ⓑ Leg
- Ⓒ Eight
- **Ⓓ Animal**

6 The word multicolored is based on the Latin root multi-, which means "many." Based on this, what does multicolored mean?

- Ⓐ Something that is bright
- **Ⓑ Something with more than one color**
- Ⓒ Something that is nice to look at
- Ⓓ Something that is shared

7 Which of the following measures time?

- Ⓐ Chronometer
- Ⓑ Thermometer
- **Ⓒ Speedometer**
- Ⓓ Micrometer

Quiz 6: Use a Dictionary or Glossary

1 What is the correct way to divide <u>visitor</u> into syllables?

    Ⓐ   vis-i-tor

    Ⓑ   visit-or

    Ⓒ   vi-sit-or

    Ⓓ   vis-it-or

2 How should the word <u>remember</u> be divided into syllables?

    Ⓐ   re-mem-ber

    Ⓑ   re-memb-er

    Ⓒ   re-me-mb-er

    Ⓓ   rem-em-ber

3 Read this dictionary entry for the word <u>concert</u>.

> **concert** [kon-surt]
> *noun*
> 1. a public performance of music

What does "[kon-surt]" in the entry explain?

    Ⓐ   What the word means

    Ⓑ   What type of word it is

    Ⓒ   How to say the word

    Ⓓ   Where the word comes from

4 Read this dictionary entry for the word crest.

> **crest** *noun*
> 1. the top of a mountain or hill 2. the top of a wave 3. a growth of feathers or fur on the head of a bird or reptile 4. a ridge on the neck of an animal

Which definition of the word crest is used in the sentence below?

The hikers looked up and were disappointed that the crest still seemed miles away.

- Ⓐ Definition 1
- Ⓑ Definition 2
- Ⓒ Definition 3
- Ⓓ Definition 4

5 Read this dictionary entry for the word dull.

> **dull** *adjective*
> 1. not sharp, blunt 2. causing boredom 3. not bright, dim 4. having little color

Which definition of the word dull is used in the sentence below?

Teresa found the long talk about the history of the museum dull.

- Ⓐ Definition 1
- Ⓑ Definition 2
- Ⓒ Definition 3
- Ⓓ Definition 4

Section 3: Reading Practice Test 1

INTRODUCTION TO THE READING PRACTICE TEST
For Parents, Teachers, and Tutors

How Reading is Assessed by the State of Texas

The STAAR Reading test assesses reading skills by having students read literary and informational passages and answer questions about the passages. On the actual STAAR test, students will read 4 or 5 individual passages, as well as 1 or 2 sets of paired passages. Students will answer a total of 42 multiple-choice questions.

About the STAAR Reading Practice Test

This section of the book contains a practice test similar to the real STAAR Reading test. To ensure that all skills are tested, it is slightly longer than the real test. It has 5 individual passages, 1 set of paired passages, and a total of 52 questions. The questions cover all the skills tested on the STAAR Reading test, and have the same formats.

Taking the Test

Students are given 4 hours to complete the actual STAAR Reading test. Individual schools are allowed to determine their own schedule, though the test must be completed on the same school day. Schools may choose to include breaks or to complete the test in two or more sessions.

This practice test is designed to be taken in two sessions of 2 hours each. You can use the same time limit, or you can choose not to time the test. In real testing situations, students will complete the two sessions on the same day. You can follow this schedule, or you can choose your own schedule.

Students complete the STAAR Reading test by marking their answers on an answer sheet. An answer sheet is included in the back of the book.

Reading Skills

The STAAR Reading test assesses a specific set of skills. These skills are described in the TEKS, or Texas Essential Knowledge and Skills. The full answer key at the end of the book identifies the specific skill that each question is testing.

STAAR Reading

Practice Test 1

Session 1

Instructions

Read the passages. Each passage is followed by questions.

Read each question carefully. Then select the best answer. Fill in the circle for the best answer.

The West Moor Sports Camp

The health of our children is important. Good health means eating well and being active. Children should take part in sports or other activities often. This isn't always easy. In cities, it can be hard to find activities to do. Don't be alarmed, though. The West Moor Sports Camp can help!

The West Moor Sports Camp is an outdoor camp for people of all ages. Children can enjoy outdoor activities. They can also make new friends. All while the parents relax, knowing that their children are safe.

The West Moor Sports Camp is located among lush fields. There is a lot of open space for youngsters to run around and enjoy themselves. There are many games and sports that they can take part in. These include football, soccer, baseball, basketball, athletics, and tennis. They can also take part in activities on the lake like rowing and sailing. There are also fitness classes that children can take part in.

There are many benefits to the camp. The first is that children will take part in a fitness program that they will enjoy! They will become fitter while having fun! The second is that children will make new friends. They will learn how to work with other children. It may also help children develop good fitness habits. Finally, children will have the chance to try activities they might never have been able to do before. Children can have a go at everything. With so many to choose from, they might find the sport or hobby that is just right for them.

Many children find that they enjoy playing sports. They leave our camp with a new appreciation for being outdoors and being active. It becomes a new interest. In the age of computer games, this is a great thing!

So visit our website today to find out more. Give your children a better future!

Practice Test Book, STAAR Reading, Grade 4

1 Read this dictionary entry for the word hard.

> **hard** *adjective*
> 1. solid and firm 2. difficult to do 3. difficult to understand
> 4. strong in force

Which definition of the word hard is used in the sentence below?

In cities, it can be hard to find activities to do.

- Ⓐ Definition 1
- Ⓑ Definition 2
- Ⓒ Definition 3
- Ⓓ Definition 4

2 In the first paragraph, what does the word alarmed mean?
- Ⓐ Worried
- Ⓑ Lazy
- Ⓒ Confused
- Ⓓ Silly

3 How is the first paragraph mainly organized?
- Ⓐ A problem is described and then a solution is given.
- Ⓑ Events are described in the order they occur.
- Ⓒ Facts are given to support an argument.
- Ⓓ A question is asked and then answered.

4 According to the passage, which sport can be added to the web below?

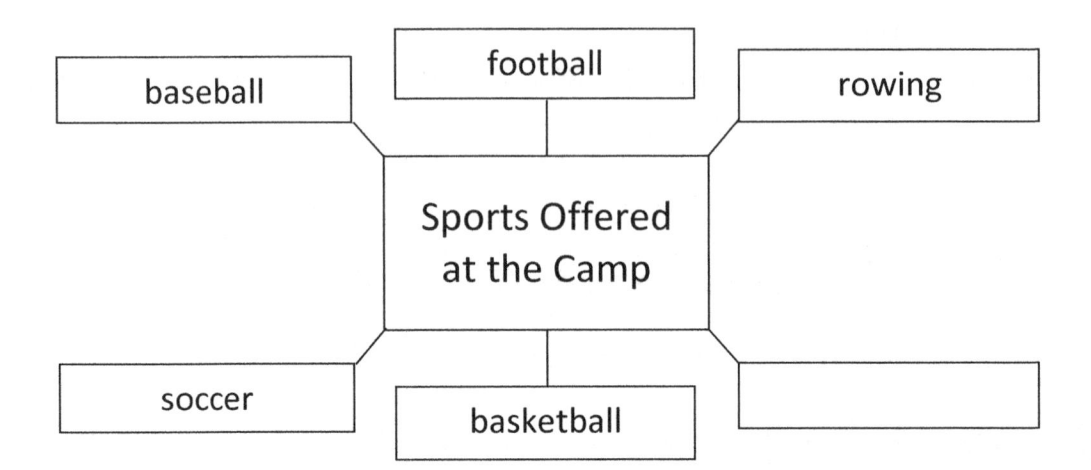

```
        football
baseball          rowing
     Sports Offered
       at the Camp
  soccer        
        basketball
```

- Ⓐ Golf
- Ⓑ Tennis
- Ⓒ Swimming
- Ⓓ Volleyball

5 The photograph is probably included mainly as an example of children –
- Ⓐ being looked after
- Ⓑ making new friends
- Ⓒ solving problems
- Ⓓ working together

6 Which question is the passage mainly intended to answer?
- Ⓐ When was the West Moor Sports Camp started?
- Ⓑ What skills do young people need to develop?
- Ⓒ Why should children attend the West Moor Sports Camp?
- Ⓓ Will the West Moor Sports Camp be safe for kids?

7 According to the passage, what should you do to find out more about the camp?

- Ⓐ Request a brochure
- Ⓑ Telephone the camp
- Ⓒ Attend an open day
- Ⓓ Visit the camp's website

8 Which of these is NOT a benefit of the camp that could complete the diagram below?

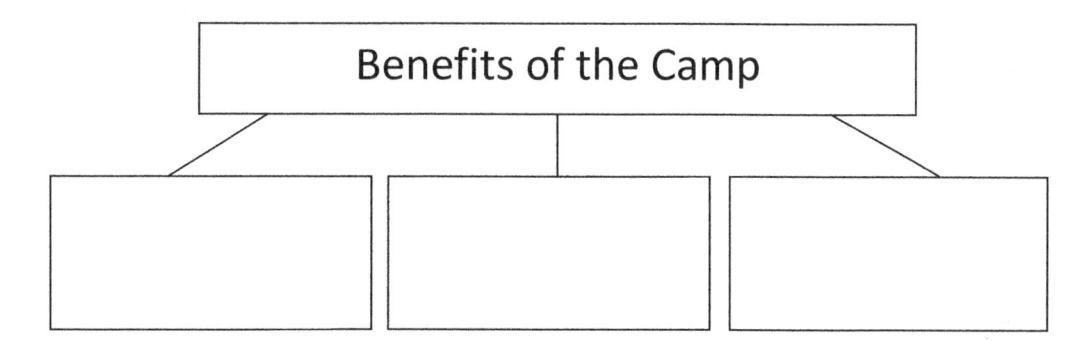

```
        Benefits of the Camp
        /        |        \
    [     ]   [     ]   [     ]
```

- Ⓐ Children make friends.
- Ⓑ Children become fitter.
- Ⓒ Children learn to eat better.
- Ⓓ Children become interested in sports.

9 Which sentence is included mainly to persuade the reader?

- Ⓐ *The West Moor Sports Camp is an outdoor camp for people of all ages.*
- Ⓑ *There are many games and sports that they can take part in.*
- Ⓒ *Many children find that they enjoy playing sports.*
- Ⓓ *Give your children a better future!*

Keep Smiling

Happiness is something special,
To be enjoyed by young and old,
And then be shared by one another,
To keep us warm through winter's cold.

Whatever time or season,
Or hour of the day,
Happiness can lift your spirits,
More than words could ever say.

And turn your sadness into joy,
Make a smile from a frown.
It brings a burst of gentle laughter,
And lifts you up when you are down.

Without it life is nothing,
Just a pale shade of gray.
An everlasting stretch of nighttime,
That waits patiently for day.

So make the most of living,
And make happiness your friend.
Greet it warmly and keep smiling,
Keep happiness close until your end.

And never doubt its power,
To bring enjoyment out of sorrow,
And leave you smiling through your slumber,
As you wait to greet tomorrow.

10   What does the word <u>sorrow</u> most likely mean in the line below?

   To bring enjoyment out of sorrow,

   Ⓐ   Boredom

   Ⓑ   Problems

   Ⓒ   Sadness

   Ⓓ   Peace

11   What does the line below mean?

   Happiness can lift your spirits,

   Ⓐ   Happiness can be hard to find.

   Ⓑ   Happiness can make you feel better.

   Ⓒ   Happiness can feel like floating.

   Ⓓ   Happiness can bring people closer.

12   The poet describes how life can be "just a pale shade of gray" to show that life can be –

   Ⓐ   simple

   Ⓑ   weird

   Ⓒ   boring

   Ⓓ   difficult

13 Read this line from the poem.

> **It brings a burst of gentle laughter,**

Which literary technique does the poet use to help the reader imagine sudden laughter?

- Ⓐ Alliteration
- Ⓑ Simile
- Ⓒ Metaphor
- Ⓓ Flashback

14 What is the rhyme pattern of each stanza of the poem?

- Ⓐ All the lines rhyme with each other.
- Ⓑ There are two pairs of rhyming lines.
- Ⓒ The second and fourth lines rhyme.
- Ⓓ None of the lines rhyme.

15 What type of poem is "Keep Smiling"?

- Ⓐ Rhyming
- Ⓑ Free verse
- Ⓒ Limerick
- Ⓓ Sonnet

16 Which statement best describes the theme of the poem?

- Ⓐ You should have fun while you are young.
- Ⓑ Every day is a chance to try something new.
- Ⓒ It is important to be happy and enjoy life.
- Ⓓ There is no time like the present.

17 Hyperbole is the use of exaggeration to make a point. Which line from the poem contains hyperbole?

- Ⓐ *To be enjoyed by young and old,*
- Ⓑ *Make a smile from a frown.*
- Ⓒ *An everlasting stretch of nighttime,*
- Ⓓ *As you wait to greet tomorrow.*

Muhammad Ali

Muhammad Ali is a famous American boxer. He was born in 1942. Many people believe that he is the greatest boxer of all time. Ali won the World Heavyweight Championship three times. He fought on four different continents. He had his first success as an amateur boxer. In 1960, he won an Olympic gold medal. During this time, he was known as Cassius Clay. He changed his name in 1964.

Ali became known as a fast and powerful fighter. He was also very confident. He often predicted which round he would win each fight. Some people thought he should be more humble, while others loved his attitude. He won his first title in 1964 after beating the fearsome Sonny Liston. Ali defended his title several times. By 1967, he was considered to be unbeatable. Then the Vietnam War occurred. Ali was meant to go to war, but he refused. He was unfairly stripped of his World Heavyweight Champion title. He was arrested and had his boxing license taken away. He fought the charges. He won his right to freedom. He also won the right to box again. In 1971, he continued his career.

He had lost some of his speed and power. However, he still reclaimed his title twice. He had famous bouts with Joe Frazier and George Foreman. He won both of these fights. His last fight was against Trevor Berbick in 1981. He was not as quick as usual, and he lost the fight.

He retired with a career record of 56 wins and 5 defeats. Ali now spends much of his time working with charities. In 1996, the Olympics were held in Atlanta. Ali was chosen to light the torch. It was a great way to honor a great sportsman.

His honors have not only been given to him for his sporting achievements. In 1999, he was awarded the Presidential Medal of Freedom. This is the highest medal an American civilian can receive. He was awarded the medal not only because of his sporting successes, but for his service to others and his efforts in promoting peace and equality. When awarding him the medal, President George W. Bush described Ali as "a fierce fighter and a man of peace." This is a good way to sum up Ali's achievements.

18 Read this sentence from the passage.

Ali became known as a fast and powerful fighter.

Which word means about the same as powerful?

- Ⓐ Angry
- Ⓑ Quick
- Ⓒ Skilled
- Ⓓ Strong

19 In the third paragraph, what does the word reclaimed mean?

- Ⓐ Less claimed
- Ⓑ Not claimed
- Ⓒ Claimed again
- Ⓓ Claimed before

20 Who did Ali defeat to win his first boxing title?

- Ⓐ Sonny Liston
- Ⓑ Joe Frazier
- Ⓒ George Foreman
- Ⓓ Trevor Berbick

21 The passage is most like –

Ⓐ a biography

Ⓑ an advertisement

Ⓒ an autobiography

Ⓓ a news article

22 Which detail from the passage is least important to the main idea?

Ⓐ Ali is thought of as the greatest boxer of all time.

Ⓑ Ali fought on four different continents.

Ⓒ Ali won his first world title in 1964.

Ⓓ Ali had 56 wins and 5 defeats.

23 Which sentence from the passage is an opinion?

Ⓐ *In 1960, he won an Olympic gold medal.*

Ⓑ *During this time, he was known as Cassius Clay.*

Ⓒ *His last fight was against Trevor Berbick in 1981.*

Ⓓ *It was a great way to honor a great sportsman.*

24 Which sentence from the passage best supports the idea that Ali was a successful boxer?

Ⓐ *Ali won the World Heavyweight Championship three times.*

Ⓑ *During this time, he was known as Cassius Clay.*

Ⓒ *He often predicted which round he would win each fight.*

Ⓓ *Ali now spends much of his time working with charities.*

25 How is the passage mainly organized?

- Ⓐ A problem is described and then a solution is given.
- Ⓑ Events are described in the order they occurred.
- Ⓒ Facts are given to support an argument.
- Ⓓ A question is asked and then answered.

26 The passage describes how actions were taken against Ali when he refused to take part in the Vietnam War. Which of the following should NOT be added to the web to summarize the actions taken?

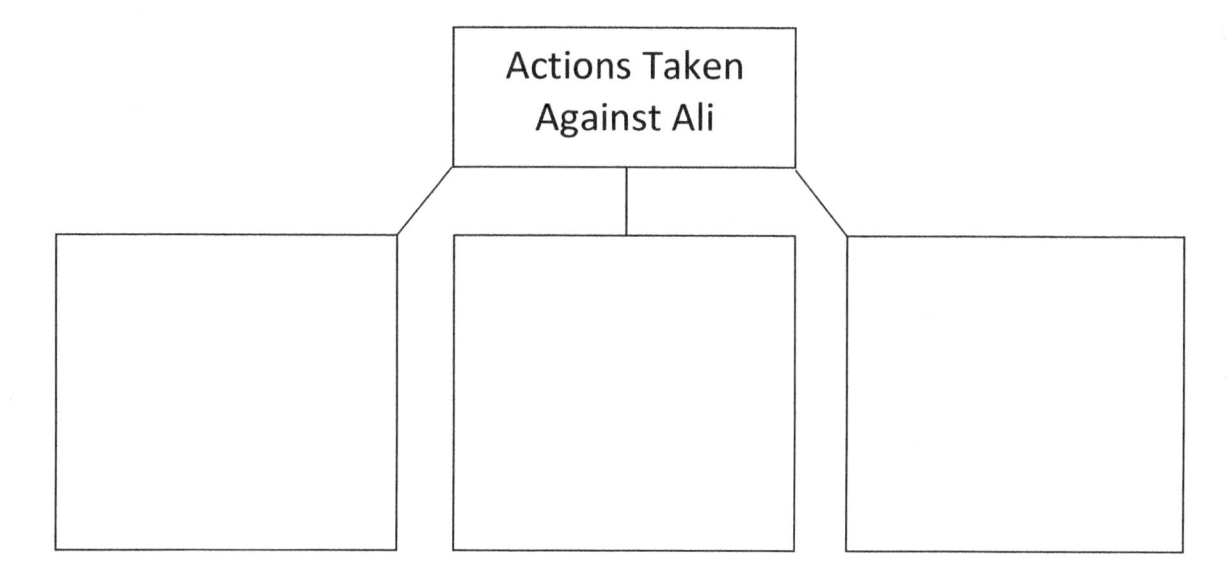

```
            ┌──────────────────┐
            │  Actions Taken   │
            │   Against Ali    │
            └──────────────────┘
           /         |         \
    ┌─────┐     ┌─────────┐     ┌─────┐
    │     │     │         │     │     │
    └─────┘     └─────────┘     └─────┘
```

- Ⓐ He was arrested.
- Ⓑ He was stripped of his World Heavyweight Champion title.
- Ⓒ He had his Olympic medal taken from him.
- Ⓓ He had his boxing license taken away.

END OF SESSION 1

STAAR Reading

Practice Test 1

Session 2

Instructions

Read the passages. Each passage is followed by questions.

Read each question carefully. Then select the best answer. Fill in the circle for the best answer.

Beneath the Silver Stars

It was fair to say that Lucas was sometimes mean to his younger sister. He would often play practical jokes on her. His parents used to tell him that it wasn't nice to scare her. He would always say that he never meant to upset her and that he was just joking. The situation was worse when the family went camping together. Lucas would play all sorts of tricks on his sister once the sun had gone down. On one particular trip, his sister Molly was having breakfast and talking about her brother to their dad.

"Why won't he just stop playing his silly pranks?" Molly complained.

"He's just a boy," her father replied. "Although, we could get him back if you want to."

Molly raised her eyebrows. Then a smile came to her face.

"How do you mean, Dad?" she asked.

"Well, I think we should play some tricks of our own," he replied. "After all, it's just a little harmless fun. We should wait until tonight and play a few little games."

Molly was very excited at her father's suggestion and thought it was a great idea.

"We won't scare him too much will we?" she asked.

"Not at all," replied her father. "When I was a child my brother used to play tricks on me all the time. It is just something that people do, darling."

By 10 o'clock that evening, it was very dark. All of the family had gone to bed. Molly's mother was fast asleep and her father was awake but quiet in his tent. At about 11 o'clock he began to hear noises from outside of the tent. He undid the zip and peered out into the darkness. He could see Lucas making howling noises from just outside Molly's tent. He chuckled softly to himself and crept slowly out onto the grass. As Lucas continued to howl, his father made his way across and hid behind a nearby tree. Lucas then paused and began to edge closer to Molly's tent. As he did so his father let out a high-pitched howl at the very top of his voice.

Lucas stood completely still. He half turned but did not want to see what was behind him. His knees started shaking a little. His father began to creep up behind him. By now Molly was peeking out of a small gap in her tent. Lucas stared ahead of him and thought about running back to his tent. As he was about to do so, his father reached out and touched his shoulder.

Lucas leapt from the spot and ran towards his tent. Molly laughed loudly as Lucas raced away.

"You see," Molly's father said with a chuckle. "Now wasn't that fun?"

27 If the passage was given another title, which title would best fit?

- Ⓐ Family Fights
- Ⓑ Payback Time
- Ⓒ How to Camp
- Ⓓ Good Times

28 Which two words from the passage have about the same meaning?

- Ⓐ *fair, mean*
- Ⓑ *pranks, tricks*
- Ⓒ *scare, harmless*
- Ⓓ *peeking, running*

29 When the father suggests getting Lucas back, the author states that Molly "raised her eyebrows." The author describes this to show that Molly is —

- Ⓐ confused
- Ⓑ frightened
- Ⓒ interested
- Ⓓ amused

30 Why does Lucas most likely make howling noises outside Molly's tent?

- Ⓐ He is trying to scare Molly.
- Ⓑ He wants Molly to come outside.
- Ⓒ He knows that Molly is going to play a trick on him.
- Ⓓ He is trying to keep animals away from the area.

Practice Test Book, STAAR Reading, Grade 4

31 How is the passage mainly organized?
- Ⓐ Two events are compared and contrasted.
- Ⓑ Events are described in the order they occur.
- Ⓒ Facts are given to support an argument.
- Ⓓ A question is asked and then answered.

32 Who is telling the story?
- Ⓐ Lucas
- Ⓑ Molly
- Ⓒ Molly's father
- Ⓓ Someone not in the story

33 Which sentence from the passage best shows that Molly cares about her brother?
- Ⓐ *"Why won't he just stop playing his silly pranks?" Molly complained.*
- Ⓑ *Molly was very excited at her father's suggestion and thought it was a great idea.*
- Ⓒ *"We won't scare him too much will we?" she asked.*
- Ⓓ *Molly laughed loudly as Lucas raced away.*

34 Which of these best explains the humor in the story?
- Ⓐ Molly is tired of her brother playing tricks on her.
- Ⓑ Molly and her family are trying to have a fun camping trip.
- Ⓒ Lucas does not really want to upset his sister.
- Ⓓ Lucas is scared by his father while he is trying to scare his sister.

Catching Up

June 15, 2013

Dear Sally,

I am writing to see how you are doing at college. Are you settling in well? I remember how upset you got when we dropped you off. I hate to think of you as being unhappy. I know what a bright and cheerful girl you are. It is hard to imagine you any other way! I am sure that you have already made a lot of new friends. How are your courses going? Are you enjoying the work and learning a lot? I bet you are finding it very interesting. I am so proud of you for studying and working your way toward your goals. It is motivating me in my own studies.

Everything is fine at home. I am halfway through my exams and have been enjoying them so far. I am prepared and relaxed when I attend each one. So far, they have all been a piece of cake. If all goes well, I may even be following in your footsteps in a few years time. We could even find ourselves at the same college. Having said that, I am not sure how much work we would actually get done! Knowing us we would either be having too much fun or wasting time with silly arguments. Seriously though, I really miss our chats.

Dad and Mom are great as always. Dad is working hard at his new job. It is going very well, and he may even have to travel to London soon. Mom is trying to get fit for our summer vacation. I know you can't make it, but you will be sorely missed. I am hoping that you will be able to make it back next year to travel with us. Any trip abroad is just not the same without you! I do understand, though. I know you are working hard and that it is all for your future.

Please write back to me when you get the chance. Until then, you will remain in my thoughts.

Lots of love,

Rory

35 Read this sentence from the passage.

I am prepared and relaxed when I attend each one.

Which word could best be used in place of prepared?

- Ⓐ Calm
- Ⓑ Ready
- Ⓒ Studied
- Ⓓ Patient

36 As it is used in the sentence below, what does sorely mean?

I know you can't make it, but you will be sorely missed.

- Ⓐ Certainly
- Ⓑ Suddenly
- Ⓒ Quietly
- Ⓓ Greatly

37 Read this sentence from the passage.

So far, they have all been a piece of cake.

The phrase "a piece of cake" is used to show that something is —

- Ⓐ easy
- Ⓑ tasty
- Ⓒ quick
- Ⓓ funny

38 What is the second paragraph mostly about?

  Ⓐ What Rory has been doing at home

  Ⓑ What Rory imagines his sister is doing

  Ⓒ Why Rory misses his sister

  Ⓓ What Rory plans to do after school

39 How does Rory feel about his sister not going on family vacations?

  Ⓐ Upset, but understanding

  Ⓑ Surprised, but pleased

  Ⓒ Shocked and annoyed

  Ⓓ Confused and sad

40 Rory would be most likely to say that he is —

  Ⓐ embarrassed by Sally

  Ⓑ proud of Sally

  Ⓒ jealous of Sally

  Ⓓ confused by Sally

41 Based on the passage, what can you conclude about Rory and Sally?

  Ⓐ They are very close.

  Ⓑ They want similar careers.

  Ⓒ They are the same age.

  Ⓓ They have similar hobbies.

Directions: Read the next two passages. Then answer the questions.

Nintendo

Did you know that Nintendo didn't always make video game consoles? Before the first Nintendo gaming console was ever thought of, Nintendo was making playing cards!

Nintendo was originally founded in 1889 to make playing cards for a game called Hanafuda. Nintendo later tried many different business ideas before finding its success. These included a taxi company, a television network, and a food company.

All of Nintendo's earlier business attempts eventually failed. It was not until 1983 when Nintendo launched the original Nintendo Entertainment System (NES) that the company found commercial success. A handheld game console called the Game Boy followed in 1989.

It has since gone on to make other similar products. The Nintendo DS was released in 2004 and has sold over 150 million units. The Nintendo Wii was launched in 2006. It was a gaming system that was able to sense the movements of players, and use the physical movements of the player to direct the game. For example, someone playing tennis would swing the controller to cause the player in the game to swing the tennis racket. The Wii sold over 90 million units in less than 5 years.

The Nintendo DS and the Nintendo Wii changed the future of the company.

Breaking In

Today, Apple is a success in the personal computer market. It offers a range of effective and attractive products. But it wasn't always that way. Apple had to struggle to break into the market.

At the time, IBM was the leader in the market. Most people wanted to buy IBM computers, and very few wanted the Apple products. Then Apple introduced the iMac G3 in 1998. The iMac G3 was one of the first real successes for Apple. Previous to the iMac, Apple saw only limited success with its earlier desktop models.

The iMac G3 came after new Apple CEO Steve Jobs decided to trim Apple's product line. He decided to focus on making products that people would like. It was a bold move and an effective one. The striking design of the iMac was just one of the reasons it was special.

The iMac G3 was unlike any computer that had been seen. The computer parts were no longer in a separate case, but were part of the monitor. The computer now looked better and took up less space. It was first released in blue, but other bright colors were soon added. The color and style were an immediate hit. Unlike the drab computers others offered, the iMac looked bright and fun to use.

Directions: Use "Nintendo" to answer the following questions.

42 The passage states that Nintendo did not find commercial success until 1983. Which word could best be used in place of <u>commercial</u>?

    Ⓐ   Business

    Ⓑ   Long-term

    Ⓒ   Sudden

    Ⓓ   Public

43 Why does the author begin the passage with a question?

    Ⓐ   To show that the information may not be true

    Ⓑ   To get readers interested in the topic of the passage

    Ⓒ   To suggest that readers should research the topic

    Ⓓ   To explain how Nintendo changed over the years

44 If the passage was given another title, which title would best fit?

    Ⓐ   The Future of Nintendo

    Ⓑ   How to Play Nintendo

    Ⓒ   Collecting Playing Cards

    Ⓓ   The Beginnings of a Business

45 The photographs are most likely included in the passage to —

    Ⓐ   provide examples of Nintendo's successful products

    Ⓑ   help readers understand what made Nintendo's products successful

    Ⓒ   demonstrate how important it was that Nintendo did not give up

    Ⓓ   show how the Nintendo Wii was different from other systems

Directions: Use "Breaking In" to answer the following questions.

46 The passage states that Steve Jobs "decided to trim Apple's product line." The word <u>trim</u> is used to show that Steve Jobs —

Ⓐ made each product smaller

Ⓑ reduced the number of products

Ⓒ decreased the weight of the products

Ⓓ made the products look more attractive

47 The author probably wrote this passage to —

Ⓐ encourage people to buy Apple products

Ⓑ describe a turning point for a company

Ⓒ analyze the sales methods of a computer company

Ⓓ tell about the life of Steve Jobs

48 Which sentence from the passage is a fact?

Ⓐ *It offers a range of effective and attractive products.*

Ⓑ *Then Apple introduced the iMac G3 in 1998.*

Ⓒ *It was a bold move and an effective one.*

Ⓓ *The striking design of the iMac was just one of the reasons it was special.*

49 What is one reason people liked the iMac G3 better than other products?

Ⓐ It was easier to use.

Ⓑ It cost much less.

Ⓒ It was bright and colorful.

Ⓓ It came with more software.

Directions: Use both "Nintendo" and "Breaking In" to answer the following questions.

50   Both of the passages have a similar topic because they describe –

   Ⓐ   the major mistakes made by a company

   Ⓑ   the influence of the CEO of a company

   Ⓒ   a company finally achieving success

   Ⓓ   a company struggling to keep up with changing technology

51   Which of these is a difference between the passages "Breaking In" and "Nintendo"?

   Ⓐ   "Breaking In" describes the past, while "Nintendo" focuses on the future.

   Ⓑ   "Breaking In" focuses on one product, while "Nintendo" describes several products.

   Ⓒ   "Breaking In" tries to persuade readers, while "Nintendo" tries to inform readers.

   Ⓓ   "Breaking In" is a biased and unfair account, while "Nintendo" is a balanced and fair account.

52   Which of these is a message of both passages?

   Ⓐ   You sometimes have to make tough choices.

   Ⓑ   There is more to life than just work.

   Ⓒ   Success will eventually come if you don't give up.

   Ⓓ   A good business needs a strong leader.

END OF SESSION 2

Section 4: Reading Practice Test 2

INTRODUCTION TO THE READING PRACTICE TEST
For Parents, Teachers, and Tutors

How Reading is Assessed by the State of Texas

The STAAR Reading test assesses reading skills by having students read literary and informational passages and answer questions about the passages. On the actual STAAR test, students will read 4 or 5 individual passages, as well as 1 or 2 sets of paired passages. Students will answer a total of 42 multiple-choice questions.

About the STAAR Reading Practice Test

This section of the book contains a practice test similar to the real STAAR Reading test. To ensure that all skills are tested, it is slightly longer than the real test. It has 5 individual passages, 1 set of paired passages, and a total of 52 questions. The questions cover all the skills tested on the STAAR Reading test, and have the same formats.

Taking the Test

Students are given 4 hours to complete the actual STAAR Reading test. Individual schools are allowed to determine their own schedule, though the test must be completed on the same school day. Schools may choose to include breaks or to complete the test in two or more sessions.

This practice test is designed to be taken in two sessions of 2 hours each. You can use the same time limit, or you can choose not to time the test. In real testing situations, students will complete the two sessions on the same day. You can follow this schedule, or you can choose your own schedule.

Students complete the STAAR Reading test by marking their answers on an answer sheet. An answer sheet is included in the back of the book.

Reading Skills

The STAAR Reading test assesses a specific set of skills. These skills are described in the TEKS, or Texas Essential Knowledge and Skills. The full answer key at the end of the book identifies the specific skill that each question is testing.

STAAR Reading

Practice Test 2

Session 1

Instructions

Read the passages. Each passage is followed by questions.

Read each question carefully. Then select the best answer. Fill in the circle for the best answer.

Robert De Niro

Robert De Niro is an American actor. He is known as one of the finest actors of his time. He has starred in a number of blockbuster films. He has also won many awards.

He was born in 1943 in New York City. De Niro left high school at the age of sixteen. He wanted to have a career in acting. He dreamed of appearing in Hollywood films. He studied acting between 1959 and 1963. He then took part in several small films.

His first major film role arrived in 1973. It was in the film *Bang the Drum Slowly*. After this, he won a role in the film *The Godfather Part II*. The film is one of the greatest films in history. He won the Academy Award for Best Supporting Actor for this role. It was the start of a great career. He was then given the lead role in many films.

During this time, he became good friends with Martin Scorsese. Scorsese was a successful director. They began to work together often. Their first film together was *Mean Streets* in 1973. De Niro won the Academy Award for Best Actor for this role. In 1980, he starred in the film *Raging Bull*. Scorsese was the director again. And again, De Niro won an Academy Award. They have worked on a number of box office hits over the years including *Casino*, *Cape Fear*, and *The Departed*.

His career continued. Over three decades, he has starred in many films. These have even included comedies like *Meet the Parents* and *Analyze This*.

In 2011, he was awarded a Golden Globe called the Cecil B. DeMille Award. This award is given for "outstanding contributions to the world of entertainment." Winners of the award in other years have included some great actors and directors including Steven Spielberg, Harrison Ford, Morgan Freeman, and Jodie Foster. It is also another achievement he shared with Martin Scorsese. Scorsese received the award in 2010.

Robert De Niro Films

Year	Title
1973	*Bang the Drum Slowly*
1974	*The Godfather Part II*
1976	*Taxi Driver*
1977	*New York, New York*
1980	*Raging Bull*
1986	*The Mission*
1987	*The Untouchables*
1988	*Midnight Run*
1990	*Goodfellas*
1991	*Backdraft*
1991	*Cape Fear*
1993	*A Bronx Tale*
1995	*Casino*
1995	*Heat*
1998	*Ronin*
1999	*Analyze This*
2000	*Meet the Parents*
2002	*Showtime*
2006	*The Good Shepherd*
2006	*The Departed*
2009	*Everybody's Fine*
2011	*Limitless*
2012	*Silver Linings Playbook*
2013	*Last Vegas*

Fun Fact

There is one other surprising link between De Niro and Scorsese. They were both the voices of characters in the 2004 animated comedy film *Shark Tale*. De Niro is the voice of a shark and Scorsese is the voice of a pufferfish!

Practice Test Book, STAAR Reading, Grade 4

1 As it is used in paragraph 1, what does <u>finest</u> mean?

Ⓐ Best

Ⓑ Smallest

Ⓒ Rarest

Ⓓ Nicest

2 Which of these does the table best show?

Ⓐ How many awards De Niro has won

Ⓑ How many times De Niro worked with Scorsese

Ⓒ How long De Niro has been acting for

Ⓓ How De Niro chooses his roles

3 Which sentence from paragraph 3 is an opinion?

Ⓐ His first major film role arrived in 1973.

Ⓑ It was in the film *Bang the Drum Slowly*.

Ⓒ After this, he won a role in the film *The Godfather Part II*.

Ⓓ The film is one of the greatest films in history.

4 How is the passage mainly organized?

Ⓐ A solution to a problem is described.

Ⓑ A question is asked and then answered.

Ⓒ A series of events are described in order.

Ⓓ Two different actors are compared.

5 The passage was probably written mainly to —

Ⓐ encourage people to become actors

Ⓑ describe the life of Robert De Niro

Ⓒ tell a funny story about a movie star

Ⓓ teach readers how to break into films

6 According to the passage, how are Robert De Niro and Martin Scorsese similar?

Ⓐ They were both born in New York.

Ⓑ They are both good actors.

Ⓒ They both direct movies.

Ⓓ They are both successful.

7 How would this passage be different if it were an autobiography?

Ⓐ It would be a more factual summary of De Niro's life.

Ⓑ It would include references to prove the statements made.

Ⓒ It would include quotes from other sources.

Ⓓ It would be De Niro's account of his own life.

8 Which detail from the passage best supports the idea that De Niro and Scorsese are a good team?

Ⓐ They met and became friends when De Niro was just starting out.

Ⓑ They have worked together on many box office hits.

Ⓒ They both received the Cecil B. DeMille Award for their achievements.

Ⓓ They each voiced a character in the animated film *Shark Tale*.

9 Read this sentence about winners of the Cecil B. DeMille Award.

> **Winners of the award in other years have included some great actors and directors including Steven Spielberg, Harrison Ford, Morgan Freeman, and Jodie Foster.**

What does this sentence help readers understand about the significance of De Niro receiving the award?

Ⓐ It suggests that receiving the award is a great honor.

Ⓑ It shows that De Niro is not as successful as some other actors.

Ⓒ It highlights that actors are only great when they have good directors.

Ⓓ It supports the idea that De Niro worked hard to earn the award.

The Change

Maria was a beautiful young girl. She had long flowing blond hair and stunning blue eyes. Maria was still very insecure about her appearance. She often thought that most of her friends were prettier than her. One day a new girl joined her school. Her name was Sarah. Sarah had wavy dark brown hair and emerald green eyes. Maria wished she looked like her new friend. Over time she became jealous of Sarah.

One day, Maria decided to take action. She thought that if she looked like Sarah then she would feel much better. So she took her allowance money and headed to the mall with her older sister Bronwyn. She visited a hair salon and purchased some colored hair dye. When she returned home, she told her mother what she planned to do.

"It's your decision," said her mother sadly. "But I think you look beautiful as you are."

Maria ignored her mother's words and headed to the bathroom. She spent several hours dying her hair dark brown. She felt much better and skipped her way into school the following day. As she reached her class she noticed a new blond girl sitting near the front. She realized that it was Sarah. Her friend had dyed her hair a lighter shade of blond. It was almost identical to how Maria's had looked before. Sarah turned around and Maria spoke to her.

"Why did you dye your hair?" Maria asked.

"Well, I always loved your gorgeous blond hair," Sarah replied. "I thought it would be cool if we matched."

Maria slumped in her chair and sighed.

10 Read this sentence from the passage.

   Maria was still very insecure about her appearance.

   If the word <u>secure</u> means "confident," what does the word <u>insecure</u> mean?

   Ⓐ More confident

   Ⓑ Less confident

   Ⓒ Not confident

   Ⓓ Most confident

11 At the end of the story, the author describes how Maria "slumped in her chair and sighed." This image suggests that she feels –

   Ⓐ sleepy

   Ⓑ nervous

   Ⓒ upset

   Ⓓ puzzled

12 Who is the main character in the passage?

   Ⓐ Sarah

   Ⓑ Maria's mother

   Ⓒ Maria

   Ⓓ Bronwyn

Practice Test Book, STAAR Reading, Grade 4

13   Read this sentence from the passage.

> **She felt much better and skipped her way into school the following day.**

What does the word <u>skipped</u> suggest about Maria?

Ⓐ   She felt nervous.

Ⓑ   She was happy.

Ⓒ   She moved quietly.

Ⓓ   She was running late.

14   How would the passage be different if it was told from Maria's point of view?

Ⓐ   The reader would dislike Sarah more.

Ⓑ   The reader would learn how to dye hair.

Ⓒ   The reader would understand Maria's feelings more.

Ⓓ   The reader would want to be like Maria.

15   What is Maria's main problem in the passage?

Ⓐ   She does not feel good about her looks.

Ⓑ   She does not have enough friends.

Ⓒ   She has never dyed her hair before.

Ⓓ   She wants Sarah to like her.

16 What does Maria do right after she gets home from the mall?

- Ⓐ She asks her sister to help her dye her hair.
- Ⓑ She tells her mother she is going to dye her hair.
- Ⓒ She learns that Sarah is also dying her hair.
- Ⓓ She goes to the bathroom to dye her hair.

17 What is the main message of the passage?

- Ⓐ Talk about your problems.
- Ⓑ Be willing to change.
- Ⓒ Listen to the people around you.
- Ⓓ Be happy with yourself.

18 Based on your answer to Question 17, which sentence spoken by a character summarizes the main idea?

- Ⓐ "It's your decision."
- Ⓑ "But I think you look beautiful as you are."
- Ⓒ "Why did you dye your hair?"
- Ⓓ "I thought it would be cool if we matched."

Happy Campers Summer Retreat

As a parent, your child's happiness is the most important thing to you. It is important to keep children healthy and active. This can be difficult to achieve. After all, many people have busy careers as well. The Happy Campers Summer Retreat was developed to help parents with this challenge.

Michael Gibson founded our group in 1998. We run a summer camp for children during the holidays. We are open from May to September. We look after hundreds of children every single year. Our staff are all experienced and fully-trained. The camp is based in the Colorado Mountains. It offers a wide range of activities for children. Our group's mission is to create a new generation of active children across America.

Our program helps children in a number of ways. It will help develop all of the qualities listed below.
- Physical fitness
- Problem-solving skills
- Social skills
- Sports ability and experience

The Happy Campers Summer Retreat can benefit all children. Some children are good at school, but rarely active. Our program will help encourage an interest in sports. Other children are mainly interested in sports. These children will play sports, but will also learn new skills. Team sports are also very important. They are used to help children develop teamwork skills, social skills, and communication skills. Children will also have the chance to try new activities. Our program is designed to help develop a complete and fully active child.

Our program is very affordable. It is available to any family in America. Your child's stay can be as short as a week or as long as six weeks. We will also cater to any special needs that your child may have.

Why not call us today or send us an email with your enquiry? Take action now and give your child this great opportunity! Our helpful staff will be able to give you all of the answers that you need.

19 In the sentence below, what does the word <u>affordable</u> refer to?

Our program is very affordable.

- Ⓐ How easy the program is
- Ⓑ How much the program costs
- Ⓒ How the program benefits children
- Ⓓ How active children need to be

20 According to the passage, where is the summer retreat held?
- Ⓐ Lake Michigan
- Ⓑ Colorado Mountains
- Ⓒ Yosemite National Park
- Ⓓ Venice Beach

21 Which word best describes how the author of the passage sounds?
- Ⓐ Serious and determined
- Ⓑ Concerned and fearful
- Ⓒ Positive and encouraging
- Ⓓ Lighthearted and funny

22 Who is the passage mainly written to appeal to?

- Ⓐ Parents
- Ⓑ Teachers
- Ⓒ Students
- Ⓓ Sports people

23 Which of these best completes the web below?

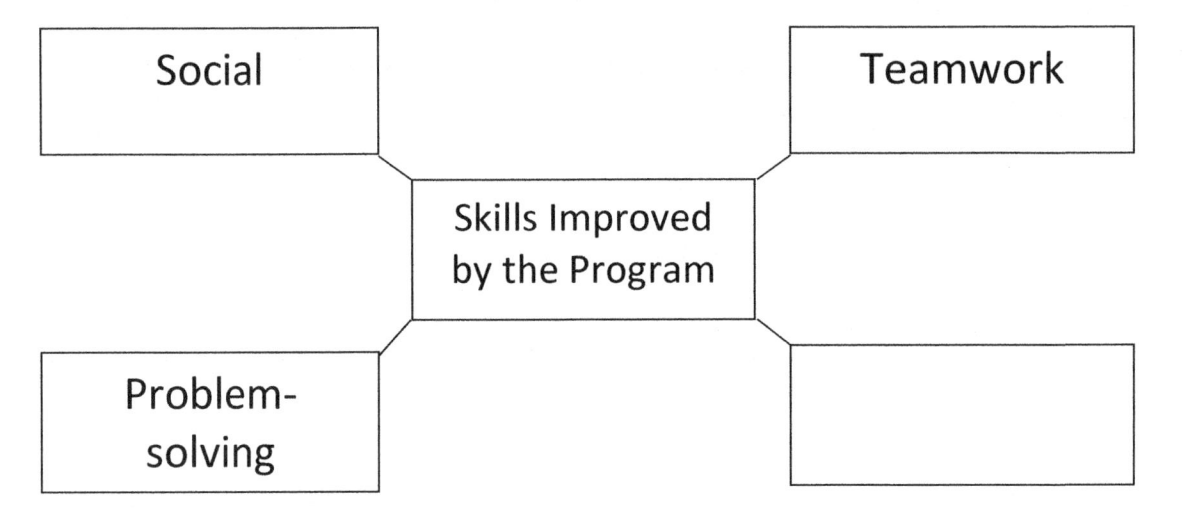

Social	Skills Improved by the Program	Teamwork
Problem-solving		

- Ⓐ Creative thinking
- Ⓑ Time management
- Ⓒ Communication
- Ⓓ Decision-making

24 The passage was probably written mainly to —

- Ⓐ encourage parents to send their children to the camp
- Ⓑ compare the camp with other activities
- Ⓒ describe the history of the camp
- Ⓓ inform parents about the benefits of outdoor activities

25 Which sentence is included mainly to persuade the reader?

- Ⓐ *After all, many people have busy careers as well.*
- Ⓑ *We run a summer camp for children during the holidays.*
- Ⓒ *It is available to any family in America.*
- Ⓓ *Take action now and give your child this great opportunity!*

26 Which sentence best supports the idea that parents can trust the camp?

- Ⓐ *Michael Gibson founded our group in 1998.*
- Ⓑ *We run a summer camp for children during the holidays.*
- Ⓒ *Our staff are all experienced and fully-trained.*
- Ⓓ *It offers a wide range of activities for children.*

END OF SESSION 1

STAAR Reading

Practice Test 2

Session 2

Instructions

Read the passages. Each passage is followed by questions.

Read each question carefully. Then select the best answer. Fill in the circle for the best answer.

Haunted House

Marvin refused to believe in ghosts. Even on Halloween, he would not get scared when his friends Steven and Jason shared horror stories. They would gather in his bedroom and sit in pale lamplight talking about ghosts and goblins. The scary stories only made Marvin laugh.

One night they were at Marvin's house enjoying a sleepover. His friends decided to test how scared of ghosts Marvin really was.

"After he has fallen asleep, let's play a trick on him," said his best friend Steven.

"That's a great idea," Jason replied.

Just after midnight, Marvin drifted off to sleep. Steven and Jason looked at each other and nodded. Steven slipped out of his sleeping bag and hid in Marvin's closet. Jason lay still next to his friend and pretended to be asleep. After a moment Steven began to tap gently on the closet door. Marvin stirred gently. Then Steven continued and tapped even harder from behind the door. Marvin sprang from his sleep and sat upright. As the noise continued, he struggled to understand where it was coming from.

"Jason," he whispered. "Do you hear that sound?"

Jason pretended to wake from a deep sleep.

"What's wrong Marvin?" Jason asked.

"Do you hear that noise?" Marvin asked again.

Jason struggled to keep a smile off his face.

"Yes," Jason replied nervously. "I think it's coming from behind the closet door."

Marvin gulped as fear gripped his body. He climbed from his bed and stepped towards the closet. He began to freeze up as he got closer to the door. His trembling hand reached out towards the door. Just as he was about to push the door open, Steven leapt out from behind the door and shouted loudly. Marvin shrieked, jumped backwards, and fell onto the sleeping bags.

"Do you believe in ghosts now?" Jason asked with a giggle.

Marvin shook his head. He tried to look annoyed, but he couldn't help smiling. Steven was laughing out loud as he sat on a nearby chair. Marvin started to laugh as well.

"Of course he does," Steven said. "But I bet he didn't expect his own house to be haunted!"

"Fine, you got me," Marvin admitted. "For just a minute, I was scared. Nice one guys. Now let's get some sleep. And no more tricking."

Steven and Jason both promised they were done with tricking. But Marvin decided to leave the lamp on just in case.

27 In the sentence below, the word <u>pale</u> shows that the light was —

> **They would gather in his bedroom and sit in pale lamplight talking about ghosts and goblins.**

Ⓐ bright

Ⓑ clear

Ⓒ dim

Ⓓ warm

28 What does the photograph of Marvin at the start of the passage mainly suggest about him?

Ⓐ He is not afraid of anything.

Ⓑ He is known for playing jokes.

Ⓒ He is more scared than he admits.

Ⓓ He is about to have a prank played on him.

29 Which of these happens first in the passage?

Ⓐ Steven hides in the closet.

Ⓑ Marvin falls asleep.

Ⓒ Steven suggests playing a trick.

Ⓓ Jason asks Marvin if he believes in ghosts.

30 Read this sentence from the passage.

Just after midnight, Marvin drifted off to sleep.

What mood does the phrase "drifted off" create?

- Ⓐ Curious
- Ⓑ Calm
- Ⓒ Playful
- Ⓓ Hopeful

31 Which words does the author use to emphasize how scared Marvin felt?

- Ⓐ "gulped" and "gripped"
- Ⓑ "stepped towards"
- Ⓒ "closer to the door"
- Ⓓ "leapt" and "shouted"

32 Why does Marvin jump backwards and fall onto the sleeping bags?

- Ⓐ Steven pushes him.
- Ⓑ Steven scares him.
- Ⓒ He is angry with Steven.
- Ⓓ He wants to go back to sleep.

33 Why does the author most likely use the word <u>sprang</u> instead of <u>woke</u> in the sentence below?

Marvin sprang from his sleep and sat upright.

Ⓐ To show that Marvin knows about the trick

Ⓑ To show that Marvin feels sleepy

Ⓒ To show that Marvin had a bad dream

Ⓓ To show that Marvin woke suddenly

34 Read this section of the passage.

"Jason," he whispered. "Do you hear that sound?"

Jason pretended to wake from a deep sleep.

"What's wrong Marvin?" Jason asked.

"Do you hear that noise?" Marvin asked again.

Jason struggled to keep a smile off his face.

"Yes," Jason replied nervously. "I think it's coming from behind the closet door."

What is the most likely reason Jason has to stop himself from smiling?

Ⓐ Jason knows that the noise is just Steven.

Ⓑ Jason is trying to seem like he is brave.

Ⓒ Jason doesn't want to embarrass Marvin.

Ⓓ Jason is scared of what is behind the door.

Baseball

Baseball is a bat and ball sport that is very popular in America. It is a game played between two teams of nine players. The aim of the game is to score runs. Players strike the ball with a bat. Then they run around four bases. When they cross home base again, they have scored a run. Home base is also known as the home plate. The bases are set at each corner of a 90-foot square called the diamond.

Each team takes it in turns to bat while the other fields. The other team must stop the batters from scoring runs by getting them out. To get a batter out, they can strike them out. This means that the batter misses the ball three times. They can also get them out by catching the ball if the batter isn't safe on a base. Players can stop at any of the four bases once they have hit the ball, which makes them safe.

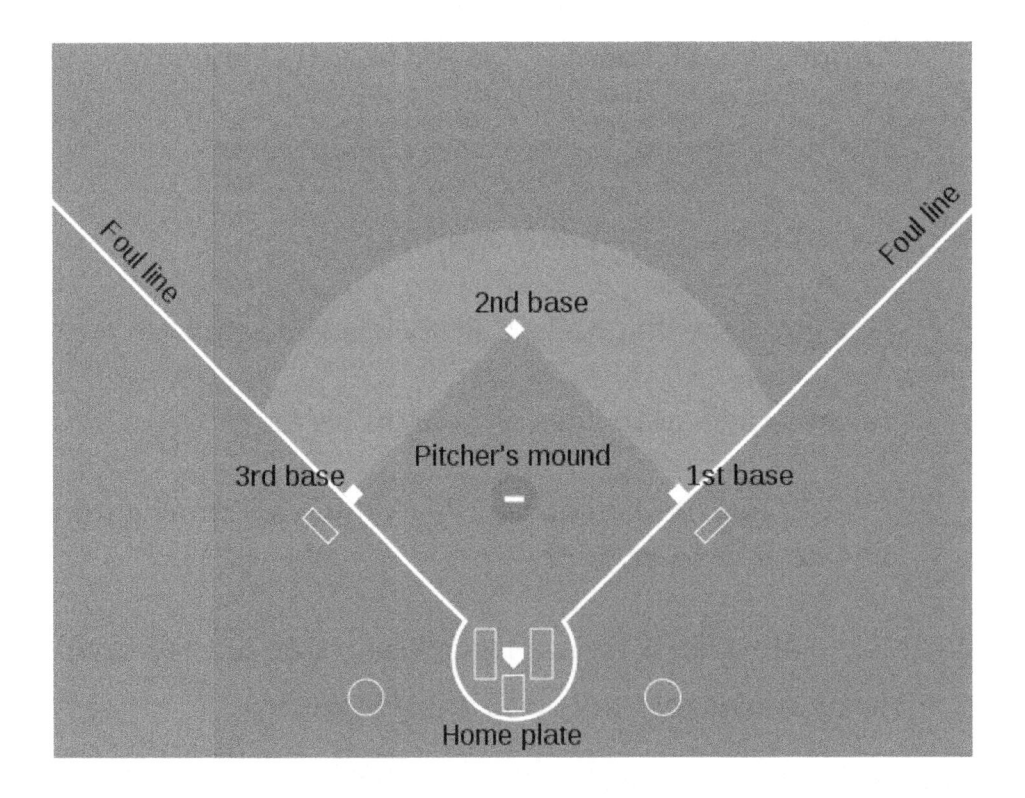

Once three players are out, the fielding team takes their turn to bat. Each time a team bats, it is known as an innings. There are nine innings in a professional league game. The team that scores the most runs at the close of all innings is the winner. The player who throws the ball to the batting team is known as the pitcher. Each professional game has at least two umpires who ensure fair play between the teams. Some big games have six umpires. There is one at each base and another two along the foul lines. The umpires know that their decisions could change the game, so they watch their areas closely.

The umpires judge whether players on the batting team are out or not. This usually means working out whether the player touched the base before the fielder touched the base with the ball. Umpires also decide whether or not pitchers throw the ball correctly. For example, a pitcher must have one foot on the pitcher's mound at the start of every pitch. The umpires also judge whether each pitch passes through the batter's strike zone. If the ball does pass through, the pitch will count as a strike even if the batter does not swing. If the ball is too high or too wide, it is counted as a ball.

The umpire watches closely. If the runner reaches the base before the fielder receives the ball, he will be safe and will not be out.

Baseball developed from the traditional bat and ball games of the 18th century. It has a sister sport referred to as rounders. Both of these sports were first played in America by British and Irish immigrants. It has since developed to become known as the national sport of North America. Over the last 20 years, the sport has also grown worldwide. It is now very popular in the Caribbean, South America, and many parts of Asia.

Baseball is a great sport for young kids. It is safer than contact sports like football. It requires a range of skills. Players can focus on being good batters, pitchers, or fielders. At the same time, players learn to work together as a team.

35 Which meaning of the word <u>fair</u> is used in the sentence below?

Each professional game has at least two umpires who ensure fair play between the teams.

- Ⓐ Average
- Ⓑ Just or correct
- Ⓒ Pale
- Ⓓ Sunny or clear

36 What is the player who throws the ball to the batting team called?
- Ⓐ Bowler
- Ⓑ Runner
- Ⓒ Catcher
- Ⓓ Pitcher

37 Which sentence from the passage is an opinion?
- Ⓐ *It is a game played between two teams of nine players.*
- Ⓑ *Each time a team bats, it is known as an innings.*
- Ⓒ *Over the last 20 years, the sport has also grown worldwide.*
- Ⓓ *It is safer than contact sports like football.*

38 What does the diagram most help the reader understand?
- Ⓐ How many players are on a team
- Ⓑ The main rules of baseball
- Ⓒ Where the bases are located
- Ⓓ What the purpose of the pitcher is

39 The passage was probably written mainly to –

- Ⓐ encourage people to play sport
- Ⓑ teach readers about the sport of baseball
- Ⓒ show why baseball is popular
- Ⓓ describe the history of baseball

40 Read this sentence from the passage.

Players strike the ball with a bat.

Which word could best be used in place of <u>strike</u>?

- Ⓐ Swap
- Ⓑ Shove
- Ⓒ Hit
- Ⓓ Throw

41 How does the photograph help explain why an umpire is placed at each base in big games?

- Ⓐ It shows how important the decision is to the game.
- Ⓑ It shows that players can try to cheat.
- Ⓒ It shows that it can be hard to judge whether the runner is safe.
- Ⓓ It shows how far the player runs between bases.

Vacation Time

Quinn, Harley, and Max were sitting beside the basketball court eating lunch.

"What are you doing this summer, Harley?" Quinn asked.

"Well, I'll probably go to see my grandparents in Florida," Harley replied. "What about you?"

"That sounds like fun. I'm probably going to go visit my Dad in Australia!" Quinn said.

"What about you?" Quinn asked Max.

"I'm going to stay here in town," Max said.

Quinn and Harley both shook their heads sadly.

"Well, that sounds awfully boring," Harley said.

Max tilted his head a little and thought for a moment.

"Well, I'm going to watch television, play basketball, go to the local swimming pool, ride my bike, play computer games, read some books..."

Max went on and on and listed even more things he was going to do.

Quinn stared at Max, "Oh boy, is that all?"

The boys laughed and ate the rest of their lunch.

Fish Food

"Come on, it's not that far now!" Sam yelled.

Ben wiped away some sweat and kept going. It was a very warm day, and it just kept getting warmer.

Sam and Ben were on their way to the big lake to catch some fish. They had their fishing rods and some bait to put on their hooks.

They finally found a good spot near the lake. They sat down to start fishing. Ben opened the ice cream container where he had asked his mother to put the bait.

"This is not fishing bait. These worms are made of candy!" Ben said. "I should have told Mom I wanted worms to use as bait."

"We could still try," Sam offered. "Maybe the fish will like the candy worms."

Ben wasn't sure it would work, but it sounded like fun. He didn't mind if they didn't catch anything anyway. He just liked sitting back and enjoying a lazy afternoon by the lake.

"It's worth a try," Ben said. "But we should keep a few worms for ourselves."

Directions: Use "Vacation Time" to answer the following questions.

42. Which statement is most likely true about Max?
    - Ⓐ He wishes he could visit Australia.
    - Ⓑ He is looking forward to summer.
    - Ⓒ He thinks summer will be boring.
    - Ⓓ He wants his friends to stay in town.

43. What is the passage mainly about?
    - Ⓐ Three boys discussing their vacations
    - Ⓑ Three boys trying to think of something fun to do
    - Ⓒ Three boys playing basketball together
    - Ⓓ Three boys arguing about what to do together

44. In which sentence from the passage is the character being humorous?
    - Ⓐ "What are you doing this summer, Harley?" Quinn asked.
    - Ⓑ "I'm going to stay here in town," Max said.
    - Ⓒ "Well, that sounds awfully boring," Harley said.
    - Ⓓ Quinn stared at Max, "Oh boy, is that all?"

45. What does the photograph in the passage represent?
    - Ⓐ What Quinn and Harley will miss most when they are away
    - Ⓑ Where the boys are talking about their summers
    - Ⓒ How you can do fun things on your own
    - Ⓓ One of the things Max plans to do over summer

Directions: Use "Fish Food" to answer the following questions.

46. What will Sam and Ben most likely do next?
    - Ⓐ   Start eating the candy worms
    - Ⓑ   Start fishing using the candy worms
    - Ⓒ   Choose a different spot to fish
    - Ⓓ   Decide to go home and do something else

47. What is the most likely reason Ben's mother put candy in the ice cream container?
    - Ⓐ   She thought that they would make good bait.
    - Ⓑ   She didn't realize that Ben wanted worms for bait.
    - Ⓒ   She didn't want Sam and Ben to catch any fish.
    - Ⓓ   She wanted Sam and Ben to have a snack to eat.

48. What happens right after Ben opens the ice cream container?
    - Ⓐ   He sees that he has candy worms.
    - Ⓑ   He finds a good fishing spot.
    - Ⓒ   He decides to fish anyway.
    - Ⓓ   He asks his mother to pack the bait.

49. The photograph in the passage mainly makes the lake seem like –
    - Ⓐ   a busy place
    - Ⓑ   an exciting place
    - Ⓒ   a peaceful place
    - Ⓓ   a lonely place

Directions: Use both "Vacation Time" and "Fish Food" to answer the following questions.

50. In what way are Max and Ben similar?
    - Ⓐ They are both jealous of their friends.
    - Ⓑ They both long for adventure.
    - Ⓒ They both want others to like them.
    - Ⓓ They are both positive and easygoing.

51. Which main technique does the author use to tell the story in both passages?
    - Ⓐ Imagery
    - Ⓑ Dialogue
    - Ⓒ Symbolism
    - Ⓓ Comparison

52. Which statement summarizes a theme of both passages?
    - Ⓐ You should learn to laugh at yourself.
    - Ⓑ You should face any fears that you have.
    - Ⓒ You should make the most of things.
    - Ⓓ You should not be afraid to ask for what you want.

END OF SESSION 2

ANSWER KEY

The STAAR Reading test assesses a specific set of skills. These are described in the Texas Essential Knowledge and Skills, or TEKS. The TEKS are the state standards that describe what students should know and what students should be able to do.

The questions in this book cover all the TEKS standards that are assessed on the state test. The answer key that follows includes the TEKS standard that each question is testing. Use the skill listed with each question to identify areas of strength and weakness. Then target revision and instruction accordingly.

Section 1: Reading Mini-Tests

Mini-Test 1, Informational Text

Question	Answer	TEKS Standard
1	A	Analyze how words, images, graphics, and sounds work together in various forms to impact meaning.
2	A	Determine the meaning of grade-level academic English words derived from Latin, Greek, or other linguistic roots and affixes.
3	B	Explain factual information presented graphically (e.g., charts, diagrams, graphs, illustrations).
4	B	Summarize information in text, maintaining meaning and logical order.
5	A	Make inferences about text and use textual evidence to support understanding.
6	A	Use multiple text features (e.g., guide words, topic and concluding sentences) to gain an overview of the contents of text and to locate information.
7	C	Describe explicit and implicit relationships among ideas in texts organized by cause-and-effect, sequence, or comparison.
8	B	Explain factual information presented graphically (e.g., charts, diagrams, graphs, illustrations).
9	C	Analyze how words, images, graphics, and sounds work together in various forms to impact meaning.
10	D	Summarize the main idea and supporting details in text in ways that maintain meaning.

Mini-Test 2, Literary Text

Question	Answer	TEKS Standard
1	C	Use the context of the sentence to determine the meaning of unfamiliar words or multiple meaning words.
2	B	Use the context of the sentence to determine the meaning of unfamiliar words or multiple meaning words.
3	B	Describe the interaction of characters including their relationships and the changes they undergo.
4	D	Identify similarities and differences between the events and characters' experiences in a fictional work and the actual events and experiences described in an author's biography or autobiography.
5	B	Compare and contrast the adventures or exploits of characters (e.g., the trickster) in traditional and classical literature.
6	B	Describe the interaction of characters including their relationships and the changes they undergo.
7	C	Summarize information in text, maintaining meaning and logical order.
8	B	Make inferences about text and use textual evidence to support understanding.
9	B	Sequence and summarize the plot's main events and explain their influence on future events.
10	D	Identify whether the narrator or speaker of a story is first or third person.

Mini-Test 3, Informational Text

Question	Answer	TEKS Standard
1	C	Use a dictionary or glossary to determine the meanings, syllabication, and pronunciation of unknown words.
2	B	Use the context of the sentence to determine the meaning of unfamiliar words or multiple meaning words.
3	B	Determine the sequence of activities needed to carry out a procedure (e.g., following a recipe).
4	C	Describe explicit and implicit relationships among ideas in texts organized by cause-and-effect, sequence, or comparison.
5	A	Summarize the main idea and supporting details in text in ways that maintain meaning.
6	C	Use multiple text features (e.g., guide words, topic and concluding sentences) to gain an overview of the contents of text and to locate information.
7	C	Analyze how words, images, graphics, and sounds work together in various forms to impact meaning.
8	A	Determine the sequence of activities needed to carry out a procedure (e.g., following a recipe).
9	D	Determine the meaning of grade-level academic English words derived from Latin, Greek, or other linguistic roots and affixes.
10	B	Make inferences about text and use textual evidence to support understanding.

Mini-Test 4, Literary Text

Question	Answer	TEKS Standard
1	B	Determine the meaning of grade-level academic English words derived from Latin, Greek, or other linguistic roots and affixes.
2	B	Describe the interaction of characters including their relationships and the changes they undergo.
3	A	Explain how the structural elements of poetry relate to form.
4	A	Identify the author's use of similes and metaphors to produce imagery.
5	D	Compare and contrast the adventures or exploits of characters (e.g., the trickster) in traditional and classical literature.
6	C	Analyze how words, images, graphics, and sounds work together in various forms to impact meaning.
7	B	Make inferences about text and use textual evidence to support understanding.
8	C	Use the context of the sentence to determine the meaning of unfamiliar words or multiple meaning words.
9	B	Identify the author's use of similes and metaphors to produce imagery.
10	B	Sequence and summarize the plot's main events and explain their influence on future events.

Practice Test Book, STAAR Reading, Grade 4

Mini-Test 5, Paired Literary Texts

Question	Answer	TEKS Standard
1	B	Make inferences about text and use textual evidence to support understanding.
2	D	Identify whether the narrator or speaker of a story is first or third person.
3	A	Summarize information in text, maintaining meaning and logical order.
4	C	Analyze how words, images, graphics, and sounds work together in various forms to impact meaning.
5	D	Summarize and explain the lesson or message of a work of fiction as its theme.
6	C	Sequence and summarize the plot's main events and explain their influence on future events.
7	D	Use a dictionary or glossary to determine the meanings, syllabication, and pronunciation of unknown words.
8	B	Make connections (e.g., thematic links, author analysis) between literary and informational texts with similar ideas and provide textual evidence.
9	A	Make connections (e.g., thematic links, author analysis) between literary and informational texts with similar ideas and provide textual evidence.
10	B	Make connections (e.g., thematic links, author analysis) between literary and informational texts with similar ideas and provide textual evidence.

Mini-Test 6, Paired Informational Texts

Question	Answer	TEKS Standard
1	B	Use the context of the sentence to determine the meaning of unfamiliar words or multiple meaning words.
2	B	Identify similarities and differences between the events and characters' experiences in a fictional work and the actual events and experiences described in an author's biography or autobiography.
3	A	Summarize the main idea and supporting details in text in ways that maintain meaning.
4	D	Use multiple text features (e.g., guide words, topic and concluding sentences) to gain an overview of the contents of text and to locate information.
5	C	Analyze how words, images, graphics, and sounds work together in various forms to impact meaning.
6	D	Use the context of the sentence to determine the meaning of unfamiliar words or multiple meaning words.
7	B	Summarize the main idea and supporting details in text in ways that maintain meaning.
8	A	Make connections (e.g., thematic links, author analysis) between literary and informational texts with similar ideas and provide textual evidence.
9	D	Make connections (e.g., thematic links, author analysis) between literary and informational texts with similar ideas and provide textual evidence.
10	B	Make connections (e.g., thematic links, author analysis) between literary and informational texts with similar ideas and provide textual evidence.

Section 2: Vocabulary Quizzes

Quiz 1: Use Context to Determine Word Meaning

Question	Answer	TEKS Standard
1	B	Use the context of the sentence to determine the meaning of unfamiliar words or multiple meaning words.
2	A	
3	C	
4	A	
5	C	
6	B	

Quiz 2: Understand and Use Multiple Meaning Words

Question	Answer	TEKS Standard
1	D	Use the context of the sentence to determine the meaning of unfamiliar words or multiple meaning words.
2	D	
3	A	
4	B	
5	B	
6	A	

Quiz 3: Understand and Use Prefixes

Question	Answer	TEKS Standard
1	D	Determine the meaning of grade-level academic English words derived from Latin, Greek, or other linguistic roots and affixes.
2	C	
3	A	
4	A	
5	A	
6	B	
7	B	
8	B	

Quiz 4: Understand and Use Suffixes

Question	Answer	TEKS Standard
1	C	Determine the meaning of grade-level academic English words derived from Latin, Greek, or other linguistic roots and affixes.
2	A	
3	B	
4	D	
5	C	
6	A	
7	C	
8	C	

Quiz 5: Use Greek and Latin Roots

Question	Answer	TEKS Standard
1	B	Determine the meaning of grade-level academic English words derived from Latin, Greek, or other linguistic roots and affixes.
2	B	
3	B	
4	A	
5	C	
6	B	
7	A	

Quiz 6: Use a Dictionary or Glossary

Question	Answer	TEKS Standard
1	A	Use a dictionary or glossary to determine the meanings, syllabication, and pronunciation of unknown words.
2	A	
3	C	
4	A	
5	B	

Section 3: STAAR Reading Practice Test 1

Practice Test 1, Session 1

Question	Answer	TEKS Standard
1	B	Use a dictionary or glossary to determine the meanings, syllabication, and pronunciation of unknown words.
2	A	Use the context of the sentence to determine the meaning of unfamiliar words or multiple meaning words.
3	A	Describe explicit and implicit relationships among ideas in texts organized by cause-and-effect, sequence, or comparison.
4	B	Use multiple text features (e.g., guide words, topic and concluding sentences) to gain an overview of the contents of text and to locate information.
5	D	Analyze how words, images, graphics, and sounds work together in various forms to impact meaning.
6	C	Summarize the main idea and supporting details in text in ways that maintain meaning.
7	D	Use multiple text features (e.g., guide words, topic and concluding sentences) to gain an overview of the contents of text and to locate information.
8	C	Summarize information in text, maintaining meaning and logical order.
9	D	Make inferences about text and use textual evidence to support understanding.
10	C	Use the context of the sentence to determine the meaning of unfamiliar words or multiple meaning words.
11	B	Summarize and explain the lesson or message of a work of fiction as its theme.
12	C	Identify the author's use of similes and metaphors to produce imagery.
13	A	Analyze how words, images, graphics, and sounds work together in various forms to impact meaning.
14	C	Explain how the structural elements of poetry relate to form.
15	A	Explain how the structural elements of poetry relate to form.
16	C	Summarize and explain the lesson or message of a work of fiction as its theme.
17	C	Identify the author's use of similes and metaphors to produce imagery.
18	D	Use the context of the sentence to determine the meaning of unfamiliar words or multiple meaning words.
19	C	Determine the meaning of grade-level academic English words derived from Latin, Greek, or other linguistic roots and affixes.
20	A	Use multiple text features (e.g., guide words, topic and concluding sentences) to gain an overview of the contents of text and to locate information.
21	A	Identify similarities and differences between the events and characters' experiences in a fictional work and the actual events and experiences described in an author's biography or autobiography.
22	B	Summarize the main idea and supporting details in text in ways that maintain meaning.
23	D	Distinguish fact from opinion in a text and explain how to verify what is a fact.
24	A	Make inferences about text and use textual evidence to support understanding.
25	B	Describe explicit and implicit relationships among ideas in texts organized by cause-and-effect, sequence, or comparison.
26	C	Summarize information in text, maintaining meaning and logical order.

Practice Test 1, Session 2

Question	Answer	TEKS Standard
27	B	Summarize and explain the lesson or message of a work of fiction as its theme.
28	B	Use the context of the sentence to determine the meaning of unfamiliar words or multiple meaning words.
29	C	Analyze how words, images, graphics, and sounds work together in various forms to impact meaning.
30	A	Make inferences about text and use textual evidence to support understanding.
31	B	Sequence and summarize the plot's main events and explain their influence on future events.
32	D	Identify whether the narrator or speaker of a story is first or third person.
33	C	Describe the interaction of characters including their relationships and the changes they undergo.
34	D	Compare and contrast the adventures or exploits of characters (e.g., the trickster) in traditional and classical literature.
35	B	Use the context of the sentence to determine the meaning of unfamiliar words or multiple meaning words.
36	D	Use the context of the sentence to determine the meaning of unfamiliar words or multiple meaning words.
37	A	Make inferences about text and use textual evidence to support understanding.
38	A	Summarize information in text, maintaining meaning and logical order.
39	A	Describe the interaction of characters including their relationships and the changes they undergo.
40	B	Make inferences about text and use textual evidence to support understanding.
41	A	Describe the interaction of characters including their relationships and the changes they undergo.
42	A	Use the context of the sentence to determine the meaning of unfamiliar words or multiple meaning words.
43	B	Use multiple text features (e.g., guide words, topic and concluding sentences) to gain an overview of the contents of text and to locate information.
44	D	Summarize the main idea and supporting details in text in ways that maintain meaning.
45	A	Explain factual information presented graphically (e.g., charts, diagrams, graphs, illustrations).
46	B	Use the context of the sentence to determine the meaning of unfamiliar words or multiple meaning words.
47	B	Summarize information in text, maintaining meaning and logical order.
48	B	Distinguish fact from opinion in a text and explain how to verify what is a fact.
49	C	Describe explicit and implicit relationships among ideas in texts organized by cause-and-effect, sequence, or comparison.
50	C	Make connections (e.g., thematic links, author analysis) between literary and informational texts with similar ideas and provide textual evidence.
51	B	Make connections (e.g., thematic links, author analysis) between literary and informational texts with similar ideas and provide textual evidence.
52	C	Make connections (e.g., thematic links, author analysis) between literary and informational texts with similar ideas and provide textual evidence.

Section 4: STAAR Reading Practice Test 2

Practice Test 2, Session 1

Question	Answer	TEKS Standard
1	A	Determine the meaning of grade-level academic English words derived from Latin, Greek, or other linguistic roots and affixes.
2	C	Explain factual information presented graphically (e.g., charts, diagrams, graphs, illustrations).
3	D	Distinguish fact from opinion in a text and explain how to verify what is a fact.
4	C	Describe explicit and implicit relationships among ideas in texts organized by cause-and-effect, sequence, or comparison.
5	B	Summarize information in text, maintaining meaning and logical order.
6	D	Describe explicit and implicit relationships among ideas in texts organized by cause-and-effect, sequence, or comparison.
7	D	Identify similarities and differences between the events and characters' experiences in a fictional work and the actual events and experiences described in an author's biography or autobiography.
8	B	Summarize the main idea and supporting details in text in ways that maintain meaning.
9	A	Make inferences about text and use textual evidence to support understanding.
10	C	Determine the meaning of grade-level academic English words derived from Latin, Greek, or other linguistic roots and affixes.
11	C	Describe the interaction of characters including their relationships and the changes they undergo.
12	C	Describe the structural elements particular to dramatic literature.
13	B	Make inferences about text and use textual evidence to support understanding.
14	C	Identify whether the narrator or speaker of a story is first or third person.
15	A	Sequence and summarize the plot's main events and explain their influence on future events.
16	B	Sequence and summarize the plot's main events and explain their influence on future events.
17	D	Summarize and explain the lesson or message of a work of fiction as its theme.
18	B	Summarize and explain the lesson or message of a work of fiction as its theme.
19	B	Determine the meaning of grade-level academic English words derived from Latin, Greek, or other linguistic roots and affixes.
20	B	Use multiple text features (e.g., guide words, topic and concluding sentences) to gain an overview of the contents of text and to locate information.
21	C	Analyze how words, images, graphics, and sounds work together in various forms to impact meaning.
22	A	Make inferences about text and use textual evidence to support understanding.
23	C	Summarize information in text, maintaining meaning and logical order.
24	A	Summarize the main idea and supporting details in text in ways that maintain meaning.
25	D	Make inferences about text and use textual evidence to support understanding.
26	C	Describe explicit and implicit relationships among ideas in texts organized by cause-and-effect, sequence, or comparison.

Practice Test 2, Session 2

Question	Answer	TEKS Standard
27	C	Use the context of the sentence to determine the meaning of unfamiliar words or multiple meaning words.
28	A	Analyze how words, images, graphics, and sounds work together in various forms to impact meaning.
29	C	Sequence and summarize the plot's main events and explain their influence on future events.
30	B	Analyze how words, images, graphics, and sounds work together in various forms to impact meaning.
31	A	Make inferences about text and use textual evidence to support understanding.
32	B	Describe the interaction of characters including their relationships and the changes they undergo.
33	D	Use the context of the sentence to determine the meaning of unfamiliar words or multiple meaning words.
34	A	Describe the interaction of characters including their relationships and the changes they undergo.
35	B	Use the context of the sentence to determine the meaning of unfamiliar words or multiple meaning words.
36	D	Use multiple text features (e.g., guide words, topic and concluding sentences) to gain an overview of the contents of text and to locate information.
37	D	Distinguish fact from opinion in a text and explain how to verify what is a fact.
38	C	Explain factual information presented graphically.
39	B	Summarize the main idea and supporting details in text in ways that maintain meaning.
40	C	Use the context of the sentence to determine the meaning of unfamiliar words or multiple meaning words.
41	C	Analyze how words, images, graphics, and sounds work together in various forms to impact meaning.
42	B	Compare and contrast the adventures or exploits of characters (e.g., the trickster) in traditional and classical literature.
43	A	Sequence and summarize the plot's main events and explain their influence on future events.
44	D	Describe the structural elements particular to dramatic literature.
45	D	Analyze how words, images, graphics, and sounds work together in various forms to impact meaning.
46	B	Sequence and summarize the plot's main events and explain their influence on future events.
47	B	Make inferences about text and use textual evidence to support understanding.
48	A	Sequence and summarize the plot's main events and explain their influence on future events.
49	C	Analyze how words, images, graphics, and sounds work together in various forms to impact meaning.
50	D	Make connections (e.g., thematic links, author analysis) between literary and informational texts with similar ideas and provide textual evidence.
51	B	Make connections (e.g., thematic links, author analysis) between literary and informational texts with similar ideas and provide textual evidence.
52	C	Summarize and explain the lesson or message of a work of fiction as its theme.

Section 1: Reading Mini-Tests

Mini-Test 1		Mini-Test 2		Mini-Test 3	
1	Ⓐ Ⓑ Ⓒ Ⓓ	1	Ⓐ Ⓑ Ⓒ Ⓓ	1	Ⓐ Ⓑ Ⓒ Ⓓ
2	Ⓐ Ⓑ Ⓒ Ⓓ	2	Ⓐ Ⓑ Ⓒ Ⓓ	2	Ⓐ Ⓑ Ⓒ Ⓓ
3	Ⓐ Ⓑ Ⓒ Ⓓ	3	Ⓐ Ⓑ Ⓒ Ⓓ	3	Ⓐ Ⓑ Ⓒ Ⓓ
4	Ⓐ Ⓑ Ⓒ Ⓓ	4	Ⓐ Ⓑ Ⓒ Ⓓ	4	Ⓐ Ⓑ Ⓒ Ⓓ
5	Ⓐ Ⓑ Ⓒ Ⓓ	5	Ⓐ Ⓑ Ⓒ Ⓓ	5	Ⓐ Ⓑ Ⓒ Ⓓ
6	Ⓐ Ⓑ Ⓒ Ⓓ	6	Ⓐ Ⓑ Ⓒ Ⓓ	6	Ⓐ Ⓑ Ⓒ Ⓓ
7	Ⓐ Ⓑ Ⓒ Ⓓ	7	Ⓐ Ⓑ Ⓒ Ⓓ	7	Ⓐ Ⓑ Ⓒ Ⓓ
8	Ⓐ Ⓑ Ⓒ Ⓓ	8	Ⓐ Ⓑ Ⓒ Ⓓ	8	Ⓐ Ⓑ Ⓒ Ⓓ
9	Ⓐ Ⓑ Ⓒ Ⓓ	9	Ⓐ Ⓑ Ⓒ Ⓓ	9	Ⓐ Ⓑ Ⓒ Ⓓ
10	Ⓐ Ⓑ Ⓒ Ⓓ	10	Ⓐ Ⓑ Ⓒ Ⓓ	10	Ⓐ Ⓑ Ⓒ Ⓓ

Mini-Test 4		Mini-Test 5		Mini-Test 6	
1	Ⓐ Ⓑ Ⓒ Ⓓ	1	Ⓐ Ⓑ Ⓒ Ⓓ	1	Ⓐ Ⓑ Ⓒ Ⓓ
2	Ⓐ Ⓑ Ⓒ Ⓓ	2	Ⓐ Ⓑ Ⓒ Ⓓ	2	Ⓐ Ⓑ Ⓒ Ⓓ
3	Ⓐ Ⓑ Ⓒ Ⓓ	3	Ⓐ Ⓑ Ⓒ Ⓓ	3	Ⓐ Ⓑ Ⓒ Ⓓ
4	Ⓐ Ⓑ Ⓒ Ⓓ	4	Ⓐ Ⓑ Ⓒ Ⓓ	4	Ⓐ Ⓑ Ⓒ Ⓓ
5	Ⓐ Ⓑ Ⓒ Ⓓ	5	Ⓐ Ⓑ Ⓒ Ⓓ	5	Ⓐ Ⓑ Ⓒ Ⓓ
6	Ⓐ Ⓑ Ⓒ Ⓓ	6	Ⓐ Ⓑ Ⓒ Ⓓ	6	Ⓐ Ⓑ Ⓒ Ⓓ
7	Ⓐ Ⓑ Ⓒ Ⓓ	7	Ⓐ Ⓑ Ⓒ Ⓓ	7	Ⓐ Ⓑ Ⓒ Ⓓ
8	Ⓐ Ⓑ Ⓒ Ⓓ	8	Ⓐ Ⓑ Ⓒ Ⓓ	8	Ⓐ Ⓑ Ⓒ Ⓓ
9	Ⓐ Ⓑ Ⓒ Ⓓ	9	Ⓐ Ⓑ Ⓒ Ⓓ	9	Ⓐ Ⓑ Ⓒ Ⓓ
10	Ⓐ Ⓑ Ⓒ Ⓓ	10	Ⓐ Ⓑ Ⓒ Ⓓ	10	Ⓐ Ⓑ Ⓒ Ⓓ

Section 2: Vocabulary Quizzes

	Quiz 1		Quiz 2		Quiz 3
1	Ⓐ Ⓑ Ⓒ Ⓓ	1	Ⓐ Ⓑ Ⓒ Ⓓ	1	Ⓐ Ⓑ Ⓒ Ⓓ
2	Ⓐ Ⓑ Ⓒ Ⓓ	2	Ⓐ Ⓑ Ⓒ Ⓓ	2	Ⓐ Ⓑ Ⓒ Ⓓ
3	Ⓐ Ⓑ Ⓒ Ⓓ	3	Ⓐ Ⓑ Ⓒ Ⓓ	3	Ⓐ Ⓑ Ⓒ Ⓓ
4	Ⓐ Ⓑ Ⓒ Ⓓ	4	Ⓐ Ⓑ Ⓒ Ⓓ	4	Ⓐ Ⓑ Ⓒ Ⓓ
5	Ⓐ Ⓑ Ⓒ Ⓓ	5	Ⓐ Ⓑ Ⓒ Ⓓ	5	Ⓐ Ⓑ Ⓒ Ⓓ
6	Ⓐ Ⓑ Ⓒ Ⓓ	6	Ⓐ Ⓑ Ⓒ Ⓓ	6	Ⓐ Ⓑ Ⓒ Ⓓ
				7	Ⓐ Ⓑ Ⓒ Ⓓ
				8	Ⓐ Ⓑ Ⓒ Ⓓ

	Quiz 4		Quiz 5		Quiz 6
1	Ⓐ Ⓑ Ⓒ Ⓓ	1	Ⓐ Ⓑ Ⓒ Ⓓ	1	Ⓐ Ⓑ Ⓒ Ⓓ
2	Ⓐ Ⓑ Ⓒ Ⓓ	2	Ⓐ Ⓑ Ⓒ Ⓓ	2	Ⓐ Ⓑ Ⓒ Ⓓ
3	Ⓐ Ⓑ Ⓒ Ⓓ	3	Ⓐ Ⓑ Ⓒ Ⓓ	3	Ⓐ Ⓑ Ⓒ Ⓓ
4	Ⓐ Ⓑ Ⓒ Ⓓ	4	Ⓐ Ⓑ Ⓒ Ⓓ	4	Ⓐ Ⓑ Ⓒ Ⓓ
5	Ⓐ Ⓑ Ⓒ Ⓓ	5	Ⓐ Ⓑ Ⓒ Ⓓ	5	Ⓐ Ⓑ Ⓒ Ⓓ
6	Ⓐ Ⓑ Ⓒ Ⓓ	6	Ⓐ Ⓑ Ⓒ Ⓓ		
7	Ⓐ Ⓑ Ⓒ Ⓓ	7	Ⓐ Ⓑ Ⓒ Ⓓ		
8	Ⓐ Ⓑ Ⓒ Ⓓ				

Section 3: STAAR Reading Practice Test 1

STAAR Reading Practice Test 1: Session 1

#		#		#	
1	Ⓐ Ⓑ Ⓒ Ⓓ	10	Ⓐ Ⓑ Ⓒ Ⓓ	19	Ⓐ Ⓑ Ⓒ Ⓓ
2	Ⓐ Ⓑ Ⓒ Ⓓ	11	Ⓐ Ⓑ Ⓒ Ⓓ	20	Ⓐ Ⓑ Ⓒ Ⓓ
3	Ⓐ Ⓑ Ⓒ Ⓓ	12	Ⓐ Ⓑ Ⓒ Ⓓ	21	Ⓐ Ⓑ Ⓒ Ⓓ
4	Ⓐ Ⓑ Ⓒ Ⓓ	13	Ⓐ Ⓑ Ⓒ Ⓓ	22	Ⓐ Ⓑ Ⓒ Ⓓ
5	Ⓐ Ⓑ Ⓒ Ⓓ	14	Ⓐ Ⓑ Ⓒ Ⓓ	23	Ⓐ Ⓑ Ⓒ Ⓓ
6	Ⓐ Ⓑ Ⓒ Ⓓ	15	Ⓐ Ⓑ Ⓒ Ⓓ	24	Ⓐ Ⓑ Ⓒ Ⓓ
7	Ⓐ Ⓑ Ⓒ Ⓓ	16	Ⓐ Ⓑ Ⓒ Ⓓ	25	Ⓐ Ⓑ Ⓒ Ⓓ
8	Ⓐ Ⓑ Ⓒ Ⓓ	17	Ⓐ Ⓑ Ⓒ Ⓓ	26	Ⓐ Ⓑ Ⓒ Ⓓ
9	Ⓐ Ⓑ Ⓒ Ⓓ	18	Ⓐ Ⓑ Ⓒ Ⓓ		

STAAR Reading Practice Test 1: Session 2

#		#		#	
27	Ⓐ Ⓑ Ⓒ Ⓓ	36	Ⓐ Ⓑ Ⓒ Ⓓ	45	Ⓐ Ⓑ Ⓒ Ⓓ
28	Ⓐ Ⓑ Ⓒ Ⓓ	37	Ⓐ Ⓑ Ⓒ Ⓓ	46	Ⓐ Ⓑ Ⓒ Ⓓ
29	Ⓐ Ⓑ Ⓒ Ⓓ	38	Ⓐ Ⓑ Ⓒ Ⓓ	47	Ⓐ Ⓑ Ⓒ Ⓓ
30	Ⓐ Ⓑ Ⓒ Ⓓ	39	Ⓐ Ⓑ Ⓒ Ⓓ	48	Ⓐ Ⓑ Ⓒ Ⓓ
31	Ⓐ Ⓑ Ⓒ Ⓓ	40	Ⓐ Ⓑ Ⓒ Ⓓ	49	Ⓐ Ⓑ Ⓒ Ⓓ
32	Ⓐ Ⓑ Ⓒ Ⓓ	41	Ⓐ Ⓑ Ⓒ Ⓓ	50	Ⓐ Ⓑ Ⓒ Ⓓ
33	Ⓐ Ⓑ Ⓒ Ⓓ	42	Ⓐ Ⓑ Ⓒ Ⓓ	51	Ⓐ Ⓑ Ⓒ Ⓓ
34	Ⓐ Ⓑ Ⓒ Ⓓ	43	Ⓐ Ⓑ Ⓒ Ⓓ	52	Ⓐ Ⓑ Ⓒ Ⓓ
35	Ⓐ Ⓑ Ⓒ Ⓓ	44	Ⓐ Ⓑ Ⓒ Ⓓ		

Section 4: STAAR Reading Practice Test 2

STAAR Reading Practice Test 2: Session 1

1	Ⓐ Ⓑ Ⓒ Ⓓ	10	Ⓐ Ⓑ Ⓒ Ⓓ	19	Ⓐ Ⓑ Ⓒ Ⓓ
2	Ⓐ Ⓑ Ⓒ Ⓓ	11	Ⓐ Ⓑ Ⓒ Ⓓ	20	Ⓐ Ⓑ Ⓒ Ⓓ
3	Ⓐ Ⓑ Ⓒ Ⓓ	12	Ⓐ Ⓑ Ⓒ Ⓓ	21	Ⓐ Ⓑ Ⓒ Ⓓ
4	Ⓐ Ⓑ Ⓒ Ⓓ	13	Ⓐ Ⓑ Ⓒ Ⓓ	22	Ⓐ Ⓑ Ⓒ Ⓓ
5	Ⓐ Ⓑ Ⓒ Ⓓ	14	Ⓐ Ⓑ Ⓒ Ⓓ	23	Ⓐ Ⓑ Ⓒ Ⓓ
6	Ⓐ Ⓑ Ⓒ Ⓓ	15	Ⓐ Ⓑ Ⓒ Ⓓ	24	Ⓐ Ⓑ Ⓒ Ⓓ
7	Ⓐ Ⓑ Ⓒ Ⓓ	16	Ⓐ Ⓑ Ⓒ Ⓓ	25	Ⓐ Ⓑ Ⓒ Ⓓ
8	Ⓐ Ⓑ Ⓒ Ⓓ	17	Ⓐ Ⓑ Ⓒ Ⓓ	26	Ⓐ Ⓑ Ⓒ Ⓓ
9	Ⓐ Ⓑ Ⓒ Ⓓ	18	Ⓐ Ⓑ Ⓒ Ⓓ		

STAAR Reading Practice Test 2: Session 2

27	Ⓐ Ⓑ Ⓒ Ⓓ	36	Ⓐ Ⓑ Ⓒ Ⓓ	45	Ⓐ Ⓑ Ⓒ Ⓓ
28	Ⓐ Ⓑ Ⓒ Ⓓ	37	Ⓐ Ⓑ Ⓒ Ⓓ	46	Ⓐ Ⓑ Ⓒ Ⓓ
29	Ⓐ Ⓑ Ⓒ Ⓓ	38	Ⓐ Ⓑ Ⓒ Ⓓ	47	Ⓐ Ⓑ Ⓒ Ⓓ
30	Ⓐ Ⓑ Ⓒ Ⓓ	39	Ⓐ Ⓑ Ⓒ Ⓓ	48	Ⓐ Ⓑ Ⓒ Ⓓ
31	Ⓐ Ⓑ Ⓒ Ⓓ	40	Ⓐ Ⓑ Ⓒ Ⓓ	49	Ⓐ Ⓑ Ⓒ Ⓓ
32	Ⓐ Ⓑ Ⓒ Ⓓ	41	Ⓐ Ⓑ Ⓒ Ⓓ	50	Ⓐ Ⓑ Ⓒ Ⓓ
33	Ⓐ Ⓑ Ⓒ Ⓓ	42	Ⓐ Ⓑ Ⓒ Ⓓ	51	Ⓐ Ⓑ Ⓒ Ⓓ
34	Ⓐ Ⓑ Ⓒ Ⓓ	43	Ⓐ Ⓑ Ⓒ Ⓓ	52	Ⓐ Ⓑ Ⓒ Ⓓ
35	Ⓐ Ⓑ Ⓒ Ⓓ	44	Ⓐ Ⓑ Ⓒ Ⓓ		

Made in the USA
Coppell, TX
08 April 2021